Intermittent Fasting Cookbook for Women Over 50

A Collection of Delicious Recipes for Making Healthy Choices, Accelerate Weight Loss and Being Fit

By

Austin Harris

Table of Contents

Intermittent Fasting for Women

Intermittent Fasting 16/8 Mastery

Intermittent Fasting for Women Over 50

Intermittent Fasting for Women

Look Better, Fell Better and Discover a Modern Approach to Autophagy to Thrive in a Post Pandemic Scenario

By

Austin Harris

Table of Contents

Introduction

Congratulations on downloading Intermittent Fasting for women: *The Ultimate Beginners Guide for Permanent Weight Loss, Slow the Aging Process, and Heal Your Body with the Self-cleansing Process of Metabolic Autophagy.*

This book is your ultimate guide to intermittent fasting. In this book, you'll explore everything about intermittent fasting; what it is, how it works, and how best you can adapt it to suit your needs as a woman. The intermittent fasting diet is one of the best ways to lose weight since it's not restrictive but instead advocates for a change in lifestyle.

You'll notice that this book covers many facets of intermittent fasting, thus offering as much guidance you need to help you get started. This book also discredits the common belief that breakfast is the most important meal of the days hence can't be skipped. Moreover, nutritionists will tell you to eat multiple small meals during the day to stay healthy, but the intermittent fasting diet overrides this principle. The science behind the intermittent fasting is backed by various research studies that have proved that you can actually skip breakfast.

We all have a tendency to naturally fast that makes it easy to integrate intermittent fasting into our lifestyles. In fact, once you adjust to your new lifestyle of intermittent fasting, you'll be surprised that you actually don't eat as much as you think you do or you need to. Intermittent fasting will help you to not only fulfill your weight loss goals but also meet your dietary needs, fight off diseases, and maintain a healthy lifestyle.

Even then, as you read this book keep in mind that everyone's experience with intermittent fasting is different. This is the key to implementing it in your life because you'll find it easy to stick to the intermittent fasting plan that is convenient for you. It's never too late to make significant changes to your lifestyle with intermittent fasting. You can begin today.

Chapter 1: Obesity and Its Impact on Women

Obesity has a negative impact on the health of women, yet 2 in 3 women in the United States are obese. What is obesity, and how do you know you are obese? Obesity is a disorder that is characterized by having an excessive amount of body fat. It is diagnosed when your body mass index is (BMI) 30 or higher. This is calculated by dividing your weight in kilograms by your height in meters squared. Wondering what your BMI is? Can you use online BMI calculators to find out your BMI? Even then, BMI is considered less accurate in some people, especially if you're very muscular since muscles weigh more than fat. The other ways to find out if your weight is healthy is by measuring your waist circumference. If your waist circumference is more than 35 inches, then you have a higher risk of experiencing the problems associated with obesity.

Your body needs calories to work properly. However, when your body is storing more calories than its burning over time, you become obese because it means you're gaining weight. However, environmental factors can also influence obesity. When you are extremely obese, you are likely to have a myriad of health problems in addition to having low self-esteem. As a woman, you are also at risk of suffering from diseases like diabetes, heart disease, and even certain types of cancers.

Obesity Risk Factors

Although women of all ages, ethnicities, and races can be obese, obesity tends to be more common among African American Women and Latina or Hispanic women. Other risk factors for obesity among women include the following:

Genetics and family background. For some people, obesity runs in the family. This is not to say that there's a single fat gene. Rather, many genes work together resulting in your likelihood of gaining excess weight. Additionally, the kind of food you're given as a child by your caregivers and parents can influence your weight gain as an adult.

Metabolism. The rate at which your body breaks down calories will often vary from one person to the other due to various reasons affecting your weight loss and gain. When you have more muscle and less fat, your body burns fat quickly. On the contrary, when you have more fat and less muscle, you're more likely to gain weight. Moreover, your metabolism may also be affected by hormonal changes at puberty, during pregnancy, and when you get into menopause.

Trauma. You may sometimes go through life issues that you don't have control over or are not your fault that affects how fast you gain weight. Women who experience negative events in their childhood like alcoholic parents or abuse are more likely to be obese as adults.

Sleep: Lack of high-quality sleep could also lead to weight gain. This is because not getting quality sleep can affect your hormone levels, which eventually has an effect on your food choices and appetite. Not getting enough sleep may also affect your level or exercise and physical activity throughout the day.

Medicines. Some of the medicines that you may be taking such as those used in treating mental health conditions, high blood pressure, and sleep can lead to weight gain. Medicines may also make it difficult to lose weight. If you're taking prescription medicine and you notice you're gaining extra weight, don't hesitate to talk to your doctor to give you alternative medicine or ways of losing weight.

With so many factors contributing to unhealthy weight gain, you always have to be alert to know what is making you gain weight to make sure you keep your weight under control. When you're overweight or obese, it increases your risk of having serious health conditions such as:

Cancer. Women who are obese have a high risk of suffering from various types of cancer such as cancer of the thyroid, ovarian, pancreatic, multiple myeloma (blood plasma cells), meningioma (cancer of tissue covering spinal cord and brain, kidney, liver, stomach, esophagus, endometrial, colon, rectal, breast and gall bladder.

Breathing problems. When you're overweight, you'll most likely experience sleep apnea. This causes you to stop breathing or take in slow breaths during sleep.

Consequently, you'll not get enough oxygen in your body or brain during sleep. This can lead to more serious health issues like heart disease.

Heart disease. Your risk of having heart disease increases with excess weight. Therefore, you must strive to keep your weight in check in order to stay healthy and avoid heart disease that is a leading cause of death among women.

Diabetes. Having extra weight predisposes you to diabetes. On the contrary, you can prevent diabetes when you lose weight or keep your weight within the recommended range. Weight loss is also important in controlling your blood glucose, especially if you already suffer from diabetes. In fact, you'll less likely need medicine to keep your blood sugar in control.

Pregnancy problems. You might find it difficult getting pregnant when you are obese. If you're already pregnant, you're likely to experience complications like preeclampsia (dangerously high blood pressure) and gestational diabetes. Thus, you'll need close monitoring and regular prenatal care to ensure early detection and prevention of such problems.

High blood pressure. If you've obesity, you're more likely to have high blood pressure and may be advised by your doctor to lose some weight to reduce your blood pressure. When you have high blood pressure, it can damage your arteries resulting in related health conditions like heart disease and stroke.

Stroke. Being obese increases your chances of suffering from a stroke. This is particularly serious when most of your weight is around your waist than thighs and hips.

High cholesterol. When your weight is more excess, your body will change the way it processes food. Thus, your bad cholesterol increases while your good cholesterol is reduced. Consequently, the buildup of fatty plaque increases within your arteries. An increase in bad cholesterol can lead to heart disease.

You need to know when to start working towards losing weight. A 3 to 5 % loss is capable of helping lower your risk of health problems while making you healthier. Therefore, take time to discuss with your doctor the amount of weight you must lose.

Chapter 2: The Skinny on Intermittent Fasting

Losing excessive body weight/fat can be a challenge. In most cases, you'll have to give up something you love and embrace a change of lifestyle by hitting the gym. But did you know that you can lose fat, improve your metabolism, and enjoy all the other health benefits without giving up the foods you love? Intermittent fasting is an incredible solution to shedding off excess fat that comes with other benefits you'll enjoy. So, what is intermittent fasting? Although most people think of it as a diet, it is not. Intermittent fasting is a pattern of eating that cycles between periods of eating and fasting and has been proven to be effective in weight loss while sustaining the results.

Interestingly, intermittent fasting is a practice that has been in existence for a long time. What makes intermittent fasting unique is the way in which you schedule your meals. You don't change what you eat, instead what changes are when you eat. That is, instead of dictating the foods you should eat, it dictates when you should eat. Thus, with intermittent fasting, you get lean and building your muscle mass without cutting down your calories. Even then, most people opt for intermittent fasting for the sole reason of losing fat.

Who Invented the Intermittent Fasting Diet

Fasting is not a new thing. It has been practiced since human evolution. In fact, the human body is wired to fast. The hunter and gatherer population did have much food to store, and they would sometimes have nothing to eat due to scarcity. As such, they adopted the ability to function without food for long periods that are essentially fasting. There's also a religious angle to fasting for Christians and Muslims alike.

However, the current wave of intermitted fasting diet was popularized by Dr. Michael Mosley. Intermittent fasting has generated a steady positive buzz with more and more people embracing it. Dr. Mosley explains the science behind intermittent fasting. He, however, attributes the success and popularity of intermittent fasting to the fact that it's mostly psychological and teaches you better ways of eating. That is, when you get used to eating vegetables and good protein, you'll eventually crave healthy food whenever you're hungry.

Why Do You Fast

Intermittent fasting is a simple yet effective strategy for taking shedding off all the bad weight so that you only keep the good weight. This approach requires very little change in behavior. Thus, it's simple yet meaningful enough to make a difference. When you fast, a couple of changes take place in your body both at the molecular and cellular level. To understand why you need to fast to lose weight, you first must understand what happens to your body when it is in the fed and absorptive state. In the fed state, your body is absorbing and digesting food. It actually begins when you start eating and would typically last for five hours as digestion and absorption of the food you ate takes place. When your body is in this state, it can hardly burn fat due to high insulin levels. From the fed state, your body enters the postabsorptive state during which no meal processing is taking place. This stage lasts between 8 and 12 hours after the last meal before you enter the fasted state. It is during the fasted state that your body burns fat because your insulin levels are low. In the fasted state, your body burns fat that is usually inaccessible in the fed state. Fasting helps to put your body in the fat burning state that is rare to achieve when you're on a normal eating schedule.

Intermittent fasting changes the hormones in your body to utilize your fat stores effectively. Your human growth hormone levels go up dramatically, thus speeding up protein synthesis, thereby influencing your body's fat loss and muscle gain by making the fat available for use as a source of energy. What this means is that your body will be burning fat and packing muscle faster. When your insulin levels drop due to heightened insulin sensitivity making the fat stored in your body more accessible to be converted to energy, some changes in gene functions relating to protection and longevity will be amplified, and your cells will initiate repair processes efficiently and quickly. Moreover, fasting promotes autophagy that removes all the damaged cells while contributing to the renewal of cells in addition to supporting the body's regenerative processes.

What You Should Eat During Intermittent Fasting

One of the reasons why intermittent fasting is appealing is because there are no food rules. The only restrictions are on when you can eat and not what you can eat. However, this is not to say that you should be downing bags of chips and pints upon pints of ice cream. Remember, the idea is to adopt a healthy eating lifestyle. So what should you eat anyway? Well, a well-balanced diet is key to maintaining your energy levels. If your goal is to lose weight, you must focus on including nutrient-dense foods on your menu like veggies, fruits, nuts, whole grains, seeds, beans, lean proteins, and dairy. Think about unprocessed, high fiber, whole foods that offer flavor and variety. Here are some foods you should eat in plenty during intermittent fasting:

Water. Although you're not eating, it's important to make sure your stay hydrated to maintain the health of major organs in the body. To tell if you have adequate water, make sure your urine is pale yellow. Dark urine is a sign of dehydration that can cause fatigue, headaches, or even lightheadedness. If you can't stand plain water, you can add mint leaves, a squeeze of lemon juice or cucumber slices.

Fish. Dietary guidelines advocate for the consumption of at least eight ounces of fish weekly. Fish is a rich source of protein, ample quantities of Vitamin D and healthy fats. Moreover, limiting your calorie consumption can alter your cognitive ability; hence, fish will come in handy as brain food.

Avocado. It's obviously strange to eat high-calorie food when you're actually trying to lose weight. Well, the thing about avocadoes is that they're packed with monounsaturated fat that is satiating. Thus, you can be sure to stay full for longer hours than you would when you eat other foods.

Cruciferous vegetables. Foods like Brussels sprouts, broccoli, and cauliflower, are laden with fiber. Eating these foods will keep you regular while preventing constipation. Furthermore, you'll also fee full, which is great when you're fasting for hours.

Beans and legumes. Carbs are a great source of energy; hence, you can consider including low-calorie carbs like legumes and beans in your eating plan. Besides, foods like black beans, lentils, and chickpeas have been found to decrease body weight.

Potatoes. Potatoes are not necessarily bad. If anything, they offer a satiating effect that could lead to weight loss. However, this doesn't include potato chips and French fries.

Eggs. It's important to get as much protein as possible to build muscle and stay full. A large egg will give you six grams of proteins. When you eat hard boiled eggs, you're less likely to feel hungry.

Berries. You need immune boosting nutrients like vitamin c, and there's no better way to achieve this than including berries in your meal plan.

Probiotics. The bacteria in your gut aren't happy when you go for hours without food. As such, you could experience side effects like constipation. You can counter this unpleasant feeling taking probiotic-rich foods like kefir, kraut, or kombucha.

Whole grains. It's ridiculous to be on a diet and eat carbs. Well, with intermittent fasting, you can include whole grains that are rich in protein and fiber to stay full. Moreover, eating whole grains will speed up your metabolism. Think about millet, amaranth, sorghum, kamut, spelled, faro, bulgur, and freekeh, among others.

Nuts. Although nuts may contain high calories, they're most certainly important because of the good fat. According to research, polyunsaturated fat found in walnuts has the ability to alter physiological markers for satiety and hunger.

What to Consider Before Starting Intermittent Fasting

Before you begin intermittent fasting for weight loss, you need to know that this eating pattern is not for everyone. First off, you should not attempt intermittent fasting before consulting a health professional if you're underweight or you have a history of battling eating disorders. Intermittent fasting is also not recommended if you have a medical condition. Some women have also reported various effects like a cessation of a menstrual period. Ultimately, you need to be careful when you go into intermittent fasting because it has been previously found that this eating pattern is not beneficial for women compared to men. If you have fertility issues or are trying to conceive, then consider holding off intermittent fasting. Expectant and lactating mothers are also advised against intermittent fasting.

The main side effect that you'll experience when you go into intermittent fasting is hunger. Additionally, you may experience general body weakness. Your brain may also perform well. However, these are temporary, and your body will adapt to your new eating pattern over time. It's advisable that you consult your doctor before starting intermittent fasting for women if you have any of the following conditions;

• Diabetes/Problems with blood sugar regulations

• Low blood pressure

• You are underweight

• Eating disorders

• Amenorrhea

• Breastfeeding

• Trying to conceive

• Taking medications

Always look at the potential benefits of intermittent fasting before you go for it. If the risks far outweigh the benefits, this could be dangerous hence not worth trying. For instance, if you're pregnant, you definitely have more energy needs; therefore, taking on intermittent fasting would definitely be a bad idea. This also applies when you're having problems sleeping or are under chronic stress. Intermittent fasting is also discouraged if you have a history of eating disorders because it could actually cause further problems that can mess your health. While intermittent fasting has produced results for thousands of people across the globe, you must keep in mind that this is not a gateway to eating a diet comprising of highly processed food or even skipping meals randomly. Generally, intermittent fasting has an outstanding safety profile since it's not dangerous to go without food for a while when you're well-nourished and healthy.

When Do You Fast

If you're looking to get on the intermittent fasting train, you need to know when you will be fasting in order to achieve the desired outcome. There are three common ways of approaching the fast as follows:

Eat stop eat. This involves fasting for 24 hours once or twice in seven days. However, you can take calorie-free beverages during this fasting period. This is one of the best ways to start intermittent fasting because the occasional fasting will equally help you realize the many benefits of fasting.

Up day, down day. With this method of fasting, you will keep on reducing your calorie intake daily. That is, when you eat very little one day (down day), you revert to your normal caloric intake the next day (up day). The advantage of this eating pattern is that it allows you to eat every day while you still reap the benefits of fasting.

Alternate day fasting. With this schedule, you get to fast for longer periods on alternate days weekly. You fast for 24 hours and only eat one meal every day.

Lean gains. With this approach, you'll fast for 16 hours within every 24 hours and only eat during the eight-hour window. Keep in mind that sleep is included so this is not as tough as it may seem. The good thing about this fast is that you can start your 8-hour eating period at a time that works best for you. This means that you could actually skip breakfast and instead have lunch and dinner. Since this is something you'll do every day, it eventually becomes a habit making it remarkably easy to stick to it.

Chapter 3: Why Intermittent Fasting Is the Best Way for Weight Loss

Most of the weight loss diet fads will often demand that you give up certain things in order for you to see the results. Well, this is not the case with intermittent fasting that almost blends into your normal eating and sleeping pattern. Even then, the truth is that fasting in itself can be intimidating. Not eating for a couple of hours is something many people find difficult. Yet this method comes close to your lifestyle than a diet. So make sure that you identify an intermittent fasting plan that fits into your schedule, and you're able to keep up with comfortably. This will minimize the chance of having to quit because you're not putting any strain on your body.

Think about this; you fast while sleeping and break the fast when you wake up in the morning! Even more interesting, most people often fast for 12 hours and have another 12 hours of eating. As such, you can easily extend the fasting window to 16 hours and eat for eight hours to realize the benefits of intermittent fasting. Here are reasons why you should consider intermittent fasting as your weight loss regime:

Intermittent fasting is convenient. One of the reasons many people give up on other kinds of weight loss diets is because they're unable to follow through. When you have a busy lifestyle juggling between a number of things that are vying for your attention and are on a diet, the latter will definitely suffer.

On the contrary, intermittent fasting comes with convenience. For instance, when doing the 16:8 intermittent fast, you don't have to think about preparing breakfast in the morning or even lunch. Yes, you can skip breakfast.

What's more? When it's time to feed, you don't have to worry about what kind of food you should eat. Intermittent fasting is quite flexible with the foods you can include in your diet. In fact, in most instances, nothing will really change. You could even eat at a restaurant yet still enjoy the benefits of fasting.

Moreover, intermittent fasting lets you enjoy special occasions with family and friends without worrying about excess calories. However, this does not mean that you eat highly processed foods. The idea here is to develop a healthy yet convenient to implement eating pattern that can eventually be part of your lifestyle.

Intermittent fasting makes life simple. Intermittent fasting is not just convenient but also simple to follow. Whether you're always on the go or are into skipping a meal or two, this eating pattern is convenient and perfect for you. College students will particularly find intermittent fasting appealing because they can hardly find a balance between school work and maintaining a healthy social life. When you take on intermittent fasting, you'll realize there'll be fewer decisions you have to make daily. Instead, you'll have more energy to handle the most important tasks of the day. This is contrary to the effect that most diets will have on your body like feeling overwhelmed and tired in addition to being expensive and complex.

Intermittent fasting saves you time and money. If you were to go on a regular diet, no doubt you'll have to go out of your way to spend time and money to conform to a certain menu. Not to mention the amount of time that would go into shopping for the food supplies, prepping and eventually cooking at least six meals in a day. The truth is that this can be draining. However, with intermittent fasting, there's no need to get out of your normal lifestyle. If anything, it will save you money and time since you'll be having fewer meals in a day. Consequently, you don't have to spend time thinking about what you should eat or even spending a lot of time preparing the food.

Intermittent fasting strengthens your will power while improving your concentration and focus. Intermittent fasting is all about self-discipline. That is, you must learn to say no. In fact, there'll be numerous times during your fast when you'll crave food, but you must resist this urge to eat. Every time you resist this urge helps you develop your willpower as well as strengthen your ability to steer clear of distractions and temptations even in other areas of life. In addition, it'll also go a long way in improving your ability to focus and concentrate on achieving specific goals that you have yet to accomplish. Generally, you tend to be sharper and alert when you're hungry than when you've got a full tummy. This is attributed to the fact that fasting will free up all the valuable energy hence avoiding distractions while staying focused on an important goal.

Intermittent fasting lets you eat what you want and still lose weight. With intermittent fasting, weight loss is more about when you eat as opposed to what you eat. As such, it gives you more freedom to eat what you want to eat. Since you're fasting, you'll typically settle down for a larger meal and consequently more calories than you would normally eat per meal for three to six meals. Therefore, intermittent fasting is more about timing than the composition of your diet. Even then, you should avoid eating processed junk food, particularly those with empty calories since they will undo the benefits of your fast. Since intermittent fasting is more of a lifestyle, you'll do well to cut down on sweeteners and processed sugars and replace processed foods with whole foods. Ultimately, you should focus on having a balanced diet that includes whole grains, vegetables, fruits, and protein. If you're aiming at losing weight, you also must not take in too many calories during your feeding window.

Intermittent fasting helps you embrace a healthy lifestyle and avoid dangerous eating diets. Since intermittent fasting is not a diet, it's a lifestyle that can be sustained through the years. Intermittent fasting is more of a wellness revolution because it helps you to adapt to a lifestyle of eating healthy foods and avoiding dangerous diets. If you're on intermittent fasting, you should not overeat junk food; otherwise, you'll end up gaining weight. Remember, intermittent fasting isn't an excuse for indulging in your favorite chocolate cookie or ice cream without giving a care. Rather, intermittent fasting reprograms your brain so that you're accustomed to taking reduced calories than you would normally consume. This helps you to avoid the trap of overeating. In fact, you'll be surprised that over time you'll be able to say no to your favorite cookies not because you deny yourself a treat, but you simply don't want. When you're consuming fewer calories than you're taking, you'll definitely begin to burn fat and lose weight over time.

Intermittent fasting lets you have bigger meals that are more satisfying. When you have to eat every 2-3 hours, you tend to think about food for the better part of the day. Consequently, you'll hardly have big meals, particularly if you are physically inactive. Having infrequent meals in a large volume will often provide you with more calories and is much more satisfying hence a great way to feel fuller for longer periods. When you eat large meals infrequently, you'll have increased adherence to the diet over time.

Intermitted fasting helps to establish a more structured way of eating. When you are on the regular eating plan, you will, in most instances, find yourself snacking in between meals mindlessly. From a couple of cookies to a slice of cake and ice cream, there's always something you can chew on. This will definitely contribute to you gaining excess weight. Intermittent fasting helps you to structure your eating pattern without necessarily getting rid of your favorites. Instead, you eliminate the habit of eating every so often by taking better control of your diet.

Intermittent fasting improves your hunger awareness. Hunger and thirst are processed in the same part of the brain. Thus, it is common to find that you're eating throughout the day not because you're hungry but for other reasons. This can be anything from stress, boredom, happiness, or even sadness, among others. Sometimes, the mere smell of food can make you assume you're actually hungry. Thus, when you're on a fast, you'll have a heightened sense of hunger awareness that will make you realize that real hunger feels like and how to differentiate it from the hunger that is triggered by other factors.

You can still eat out and enjoy social gatherings during intermittent fasting. Unlike many weight loss diets, intermittent fasting is not restrictive in terms of the foods you need to include on your menu. So you don't have to worry about missing out on social gatherings or even eating out! In fact, this pattern of eating accommodates the social nature of human beings as we tend to build social events around food. Since most of the occasions take place in the evening, you can always stick to your fasting routine and join the rest of the gathering at the table. Intermittent fasting gives you the freedom to eat food that is served at social gatherings as well as restaurants while staying within your calorie range for the day. This makes it simple and easy to maintain. So you don't have to write off the idea of eating out.

You can still travel the world while fasting. If you love traveling, you might be hesitant about attempting intermittent fasting. However, the interesting thing is that you can still travel the world and not worry about missing new experiences because of breaking your fast outside your feeding window. You can easily integrate intermittent fasting into your diet so that you are enjoying new experiences while losing weight. This way, you don't have to eat unhealthy food or even abandon your intermittent fasting plan for weight loss. Intermittent fasting can work for you whenever and wherever you are.

Intermittent fasting helps to improve the quality of your sleep. Although most people embrace intermittent fasting solely to lose weight, it comes with other added benefits among them quality sleep. This is attributed to the fact that when you're fasting, your body digests food before you sleep. This eventually helps you to sleep better because your insulin and fat levels are better controlled. Getting quality sleep can also contribute to weight loss.

Intermittent fasting makes you feel happy. This is another added advantage of fasting for weight loss. When you lose excess weight, you will not only feel lighter but also happier because you'll be more confident in your body. Moreover, you'll also have more energy because generally, digestion often takes much of your body's energy. This is in addition to feeling more healthier and in control.

Intermittent fasting is easy to follow. In most cases, starting a diet is easy. However, many people tend to give up after several weeks of watching what you're eating and counting calories. On the contrary, intermittent fasting gives you much freedom making it a lot easier to stick with it in the long term.

Intermittent fasting helps in muscle growth. Although many people have reported that intermittent fasting resulted in the loss of muscle when done properly, intermittent fasting can contribute to muscle building. However, this will require you to tailor your intermittent fasting approach in a manner that limits your fasting period to between 10 and 12 hours so that you're not inhibiting the body's ability to build muscle. You may also have to extend your feeding window to 10 hours so that you get all the nutrients you need.

Well, intermittent fasting does more than just helping you achieve your goal of losing weight. It actually presents many other benefits that will generally improve your lifestyle. This means that you must stay committed to the intermittent fasting plan that works for you to make sure that you get the results you desire. Eventually, intermittent fasting will become part of your lifestyle.

Chapter 4: Impact of Intermittent Fasting on Your Body

A number of studies have backed up the fact that intermittent fasting presents powerful benefits to your brain and body. Some of the top benefits you'll experience when you embark on intermittent fasting for weight loss include the following:

Speeds up fat burning and weight loss. Intermittent fasting is one of the top strategies for burning fat effortlessly. Fat burning during intermittent fasting is actually a result of being in a calorie deficient state that promotes loss of fat. A study done on animals found that intermittent fasting for a period of up to 16 weeks helps in the preventions of obesity with the results being seen in just six weeks. According to researchers, intermittent fasting activates metabolism while also helping to burn more fat through the generation of body heat. When you're fasting, your insulin levels will be low. The body will break down carbohydrates into glucose that the cells will draw energy from or convert it into fat hence store it for later use. Insulin levels are low when you're not consuming food. Thus, during fasting, your insulin levels are likely to be low, prompting the cells to get their glucose from fat stores as energy. When this process is done repeatedly, it results in weight loss. Most research suggests that intermittent fasting may be an effective weight management strategy. The fact that you'll most likely be eating fewer calories than you're burning means that your body will mostly be relying on the fat stores for energy which will translate to significant weight loss.

Boosts growth hormone production. The physiology of fasting is interesting. As such, the power of fasting is not in the reduction of calories, but hormonal changes that take place. Fasting triggers increased the production of the human growth hormone (HGH) that is produced in the pituitary gland. This hormone is instrumental in the normal development in adolescents, children, and adults. In adults, a deficiency of the growth hormone results in an increase in body fat, a decrease in bone mass, and lower lean body mass. Upon release by the pituitary gland, the growth hormone lasts for just a few minutes in the bloodstream. This hormone goes to the liver for metabolism before conversion into various growth factors with the most important one being the Insulin-Like Growth Factor 1 (IGF1).

This Insulin-Like Growth Factor 1 is linked to high insulin levels as well as most poor health outcomes. Even then, the brief pulse of IGF1 from the human growth hormone only lasts for a few minutes. All hormones are secreted in brief bursts naturally ostensibly preventing the development of resistance that requires high levels as well as the persistence of those levels. This explains how insulin resistance develops. The human growth hormone is usually secreted during sleep as a counter-regulatory hormone. Together with adrenaline and cortisol, this the growth hormone increases your blood glucose by breaking down glycogen to counter insulin. These hormones are secreted in a pulse just before you wake up during a counter-regulatory surge. This is normal as it helps the ready prepare for the upcoming day.

It's, therefore, wrong to say that you derive the energy for the day from breakfast because usually, your body has already given a big shot for great stuff and fuel for the day. Therefore, you absolutely don't need to rely on all your sugary cereals for energy. This is also the reason why you least feel hungry in the morning even when you haven't eaten for 12 hours. The growth hormone tends to go down with age while abnormally low levels can result in low bone and muscle mass. Fasting stimulates the secretion of the human growth hormone. That is, when you fast, there's a spike in the morning and regular secretion throughout the day. This is critical to the maintenance of lean bone and muscle mass while the stored fats burn. When the growth hormone is elevated by fasting, your muscle mass increases.

Prevents insulin resistance. When you eat, the body breaks down the food into glucose that goes in the bloodstream for transportation to the cells. Your cells rely on this glucose as fuel to function properly. Insulin is a hormone that allows the cells to absorb glucose. Thus, whenever you eat insulin is produced, signaling the cells to absorb glucose. When the cells receive this glucose, they effectively receive energy. Even then, this is not always the case. In some instances, the communication between insulin and the cells can go off so that the glucose is not received in the cells but is instead stored as fat. This is referred to as insulin resistance. That is, as more and more insulin is produced, the cells do not respond by receiving glucose.

Insulin resistance can be caused by various reasons, yet your pancreas can only produce so much insulin before it is fatigued, leading to insulin deficiency and subsequently, diabetes. When this happens, you'll constantly feel tired, cold, and lousy. This resistance is dependent on not only the levels of insulin but also the persistence level. Intermittent fasting is a great and easiest way of increasing your insulin sensitivity. When you burn the available glucose and glycogen that is the stored glucose, your body goes into ketosis where you draw energy from ketones.

Reduces the risk of heart disease. Heart disease is a leading killer across the world. CDC puts the number of people who die from heart disease in the United States at 610,000 annually. According to research, intermittent fasting can improve certain aspects of cardiovascular health. You can reduce the risk of heart disease by making changes to your lifestyle. This includes exercising, eating right, limiting your intake of alcohol, and not smoking. Intermittent fasting restricts the calories you consume on a given day it will improve your glycemic control, cardiovascular risk as well as insulin resistance. In one study, individuals who followed an alternate day fasting plan for successfully lost weight had a notable reduction in their blood sugar levels, inflammatory markers, blood pressure, triglycerides, LDL cholesterol, and the total cholesterol. Triglycerides are a type of fat that is found in the blood and is linked to heart disease.

Increases metabolic rate. Intermittent fasting helps in improving insulin sensitivity that is key in the prevention of diabetes, increasing metabolic rate, and weight management. It's a common belief that skipping meals will result in the body adapting to the calorie deficit by lowering the metabolic rate to save energy. It has been established that extended periods of fasting can lead to a drop in metabolism. However, some studies have also shown that when you fast for short periods, you can increase your metabolism. In fact, one study conducted among 11 healthy men found that after a three day fast, their metabolism actually increased by 14%. This increase is attributed to the rise in norepinephrine hormone that, together with insulin, promotes fat burning. Based on these findings, intermittent fasting is far much significant with great weight loss advantages when compared to the other diets that are aimed to focus on calorie restriction for losing weight. Even then, the effects of intermittent fasting on metabolism are still under study because several other studies have found that your muscle mass doesn't decrease much during intermittent fasting.

Intermittent fasting changes how cells, genes, and hormones function. There's a raft of activities that go on in your body when you fast for extended periods. One of the things that happens is that your body will initiate important cellular repair processes as well as a change in the levels of hormones to make stored fat more accessible. More specifically, there'll be a significant drop in the insulin levels resulting in fat burning as the stored fats become a primary source of energy. The growth hormone in the blood may increase up to five times that also facilitates fat burning and muscle gain. Fasting also results in beneficial changes, molecules, and genes that are related to protection against disease and longevity. Cellular repair processes are also initiated when you're fasting promoting the removal of waste material from the cells.

Reduces inflammation and oxidative stress in the body. Oxidative stress is a step in most of the chronic diseases and aging. It involves unstable molecules known as free radicals that react with other molecules like DNA and protein and damage them. A number of studies show that intermittent fasting enhances your body's resistance to oxidative stress. In addition, intermittent fasting also helps in fighting inflammation that is a common cause of diseases, especially when your body is able to go into autophagy.

Induces a number of cellular repair processes. When you fast for extended periods, the cells in your body begin to initiate a waste removal process that is known as autophagy. This process not only involves breaking down but also metabolizing dysfunctional and broken proteins that accumulate in within the cells over time. Increased autophagy is able to offer protection against a number of diseases such as Alzheimer's disease.

Helps in the prevention of cancer. Cancer is a disease that is characterized by the growth of cells that is uncontrolled. Studies have found that fasting has a number of benefits on metabolism that could actually lead to a reduced risk of cancer. There's also evidence on cancer patients showing that fasting reduced some of the side effects of chemotherapy. It's important to note that these studies have mostly been done in animals; hence, there's a need for further studies in humans.

Fasting has anti-aging effects. Various forms of fasting have been found to improve healthspan and lifespan significantly. This has been demonstrated with caloric restriction in animals that reduces the number of calories by between 20 and 30%. Intermittent fasting also slows down the aging process and increases your lifespan by manipulating mitochondrial networks. Mitochondria are power generators found in the cells. They produce most of the energy the cells need for survival. Studies have shown that intermittent fasting helps to keep the mitochondrial networks fused hence keeping the mitochondria strong with the ability to process energy. This is crucial for vibrant aging and longevity. Fasting also delays the aging process and prevent diseases by triggering adaptive cellular stress responses that result in a better ability to cope with more stress while counteracting the disease. Thus, when your mitochondria work better, so will your body.

Intermittent fasting is therapeutic. When practiced well, intermittent fasting offers therapeutic benefits that are psychological, spiritual, and physical. For physical benefits, intermittent fasting can help cure diabetes. In addition, it has been proven to be extremely useful in the reduction of seizure-related brain damage as well as seizures themselves as well as improve symptoms of arthritis. Fasting also offers spiritual benefits, as is widely practiced by different religions around the world. It contributes towards purifying your soul and body when practiced within the religious context. The psychological angle of fasting is in the fact that it takes your will and self-control, which is a powerful psychological benefit. You learn how to ignore hunger and practice restraint from eating for a certain duration. This is a great practice because it's about training your mind. A successful intermittent fasting plan will have powerful effects on your psychological perspective. In fact, intermittent fasting has been proven to have positive results in women, especially in relation to improving the sense of control, pride, achievement, and reward. Moreover, it is handy for improving your self-esteem.

You need to understand how intermittent fasting will affect you before you get into it because this signals a change of lifestyle. While it may seem difficult to execute because your body is used to a certain way of eating, it's doable, and the results are incredible. The only thing you should never do is wake up one morning and jump into it. Rather, take time to prepare psychologically and begin slowly to increase your success rate, especially if you're looking to embrace healthy living by making a lifestyle change.

Chapter 5: Benefits of Intermittent Fasting

You've probably been told to make sure that you eat a balanced diet. Thus, it's odd to think that depriving yourself a meal or more can actually be a necessity. Interestingly, evidence points to the benefits of intermittent fasting on your wellbeing. Different forms of intermittent fasting will yield different benefits that go beyond weight loss. Some of the benefits of intermittent fasting include:

Weight and body fat loss. The majority of people who try intermittent fasting do it because they want to lose weight. Unlike other weight loss plan, intermittent fasting makes you adapt to an eating pattern that defines when you should eat and when you should fast. The whole idea behind intermittent fasting it offers you flexibility while making you eat fewer meals. This is not equivalent to counting calories as is usually the norm with most of the weight loss regimens. When you alter your eating pattern, then you're likely to eat much less hence taking fewer calories. In addition, intermittent fasting will enhance the hormonal function that facilitates weight loss. That is, a dip in the levels of insulin, along with a higher presence of the growth hormone and an increase in the amount of norepinephrine increases the rate at which fat is broken down into energy. As such, fasting on a short-term basis will increase your metabolic rate, thus helping you to burn more fats. Thus, intermittent fasting works to lose weight by reducing the amount of food you eat as well as boost your metabolic rate. It's estimated that you can experience up to 8% weight loss over a period of 3-24 weeks with intermittent fasting. When you have significant weight loss, your waist circumference will also reduce indicating loss of belly fat that is actually harmful.

Stable glucose level. Studies conducted in both people and mice show that various kinds of intermittent fasting can improve the way your body responds to sugar. In mice, researchers were able to reboot the pancreas that produces insulin, thereby reversing diabetes. Various forms of fasting that involve extended hours of unrestricted eating, followed by five days of eating a restricted fasting diet has been found to cause big improvements in individuals with high blood sugar. Losing weight, eating healthy, and moving more can help in fighting off the development of type 2 diabetes. Losing weight makes you more insulin sensitive hence driving your blood sugar down. When you eat, your body releases insulin in your bloodstream to supply cells energy. However, if you're pre-diabetic, your insulin resistant meaning your blood sugar levels are constantly elevated. Thus intermittent fasting can help to stabilize your glucose levels since it requires your body to produce insulin less often hence restoring your insulin secretion and promoting the generation of new insulin-producing pancreatic beta cells according to research.

Improves digestive health. The cells with the gastrointestinal tract are constantly working. In some instances, these cells work to the extent of being passed out a part of excreta. You can repair these digestive cells with intermittent fasting by making sure your body gets to autophagy. This gets rid of the old cells and activates your immune system accordingly. This also applies to a chronic gut immune response that is capable of inflaming bowels. Getting them to rest allows them a chance to restore and repair. An extended night fast and autophagy will give your gut a chance not only to relax but also recharge.

Improved brain health. Studies conducted in mice show that intermittent fasting could actually improve brain health by boosting your brainpower. As you grow older, the amount of blood flowing to your brain decreases while the neurons shrink, and the brain volume declines. Intermittent fasting halts the aging process keeping you mentally healthy and sharp. By boosting your brain health, intermittent fasting can lower your risk of neurodegenerative diseases like Parkinson's and Alzheimer's.

Furthermore, fasting reduces obesity and is able to protect you from diabetes, both of which can increase your risk of developing Alzheimer's disease. Intermittent fasting also helps in improving your brain by hindering the degeneration of nerve cells. According to one study, intermittent fasting plays an important role in guarding neurons in the brain from excitotoxic stress. In addition, it also speeds up autophagy in the neurons helping your body to eliminate all the damaged cells while generating new ones. This is important in helping the body defend itself from diseases. Your memory and learning ability also improve with intermittent fasting. Studies have shown that memory and mood are boosted after periods of caloric restriction.

Decreased risk of cancer. Cancer has become prevalent over the past few years, affecting people of all ages and race. The good news is that autophagy promises to reduce the likelihood of having cancer. Autophagy has received attention from medical professionals for its role in the prevention of cancer. This is because cancer occurs when there's a cellular disorder thus by promoting cell inflammation as well as regulation of damage response to the DNA by foreign bodies and regulating genome instability it helps to keep cancer at bay.

Promotes longevity. Intermittent fasting can help promote the overall length of life. This concept dates back to the 1950s when scientists discovered autophagy as well as the great potential it holds in determining the quality of life. That is, you don't necessarily need to take in too many nutrients to ensure your wellbeing rather, work toward promoting the internal process that recycles the damaged cell parts and eliminates the toxic body cells.

Improve immune system. Autophagy is powerful and highly effective when it comes to keeping your immune system in top shape. It achieves this by promoting inflammation in cells as well as actively fighting diseases through non-selective autophagy. When cellular inflammation happens, it boosts the cells of the immune system whenever it is attacked by diseases. Autophagy induces inflammation by depriving cell proteins of nutrition, thereby causing them to work more actively. This initiates the required immune response that keeps diseases and infections away. It also eliminates harmful elements that include tuberculosis, micro bacterium, as well as other viral elements from the cell.

Regulates inflammation. You can either reduce or boost the immune response with autophagy depending on what is required. This, in turn, prevents and promotes inflammation. When there's a dangerous invasion, autophagy will boost inflammation by signaling the immune system to attack. On the other hand, it can also decrease the inflammation within the immune system by getting rid of the signals that cause it.

Improved quality of life. The internet is awash with tons of methods and techniques that guarantee quality health and quality life in general. The truth is that none of these methods that include diets, anti-aging creams, and other products can lead closer to autophagy during intermittent fasting. The cellular degeneration and regeneration processes during autophagy are guaranteed to make you appear youthful in contrast to your actual age. This is especially important to your skin that is exposed to harsh elements of pollution as well as other substance that cause wrinkles leading to a decline in your skin quality with layers of toxic substances forming over your skin cells.

Decreased risk of neurodegenerative diseases. When your body achieves autophagy, you'll have a decreased risk of developing neurodegenerative diseases like Alzheimer's and Parkinson's. Here's how. Neurodegenerative diseases will work well on the basis of the accumulated toxic and old neurons that pile up in certain areas of the brain spreading to the surrounding areas. Therefore, autophagy replaces the neuron parts that are useless and, in their place, regenerate new ones effectively keeping these diseases in check.

Enhanced mental performance. Intermittent fasting enhances the cognitive function in addition to being useful in boosting brain power. Intermittent fasting will boost the brain-derived neurotrophic factor (BDNF) levels. This is a protein within the brain that is able to interact with the other parts of your brain that are responsible for controlling the learning, memory, and cognitive functions. The brain-derived neurotrophic factor is also capable of protecting and stimulating the growth of new brain cells. When you are on intermittent fasting, your body will go into the ketogenic state, thereby using ketones to burn body fat to energy. Ketones are also capable of feeding your brain, thus improving your mental productivity, energy, and acuity.

Prevention of diseases. Intermittent fasting has been associated with the prevention of diseases. According to research, intermittent fasting plays an important role in improving the number of risk markers for chronic disease that include lowered cholesterol, lowered blood pressure, and reduced insulin resistance. A study in the World Journal of Diabetes reveals that patients who have type 2 diabetes and are on short term daily intermittent fasting are likely to experience a drop in their lower body weight and have better variability of post-meal glucose. Intermittent fasting will also enhance stress markers resistance, reduce inflammation and blood pressure and promote better glucose circulation and lipid levels hence reducing the risk of cardiovascular diseases such as cancer, Alzheimer's, and Parkinson's. Intermittent fasting can also slow down the progression of certain cancers like skin and breast cancer by increasing the levels of tumor-infiltrating lymphocytes. These are the cells that are sent by the immune system to attack the tumor.

Improved physical fitness. Intermittent fasting influences your digestive system; hence, your level of physical fitness. Having a small feasting window and an extended fasting window encourages proper digestion of food. As a result, you have a healthy and proportional daily intake of food as well as calories. As you get used to this process, it is unlikely that you will experience hunger. You don't have to worry about slowing down your metabolism because, in reality, intermittent fasting will enhance your metabolism making it more flexible as your body has the capability to run on fats and glucose along for energy effectively. The use of oxygen is important in the success of your training. In fact, in order to perform well, you must adjust your breathing habits during workouts. Generally, the maximum amount of oxygen that your body uses per kilogram of your body weight or per minute is referred to as VO2. This is also known as wind. The amount of wind you have influences your performance. More wind means better performance.

Consequently, top athletes will have twice as much VO2 level compared to those without training. A study carried out on a fasted group that skipped breakfast and a non-fasted group that had breakfast an hour before found that the VO2 levels of both groups were 3.5L/min at the beginning. There was a notable increase in the wind in the fasting group at 9.7% compared to an increase of 2.5% in those who took breakfast.

Enhances bodybuilding. When you have a short feasting window, it automatically translates to fewer meals meaning you can concentrate your daily intake of calories in 1-2 meals. Bodybuilders find this approach to be great compared to splitting your calories in 5-6 meals spread throughout the day. You need a certain amount of protein in maintaining your muscle mass. You can still maintain your muscle mass with intermittent fasting even though this eating pattern doesn't focus on your protein intake. Since your growth hormone reaches unbelievable levels after 48 hours of fasting, you're able to maintain muscles even without having to eat proteins or even having protein shakes and bars.

Increased insulin sensitivity. Insulin sensitivity refers to your body cell's level of sensitivity in response to insulin. High levels of insulin sensitivity are good as it allows the cells to use blood glucose effectively, thereby reducing the amount of blood sugar in your system. When your insulin levels are low, you will experience insulin resistance. When this happens, you will experience abnormal levels of blood sugar, which, when not managed, will result in type 2 diabetes. Insulin sensitivity will vary between different people and will change according to various dietary factors and lifestyle. Therefore, improving it could be beneficial to those people who are living with or are at risk of developing type 2 diabetes. According to a 2014 review investigating the effect of intermittent fasting in obese and overweight adults, intermittent fasting has the ability to reduce insulin resistance. Even then, there was no significant effect on glucose levels.

Intermittent fasting will provide amazing results when done right. From the loss of excessive weight to a reversal of type 2 diabetes, many benefits are linked to intermittent fasting. Even then, you need to stay committed and be consistent with your intermittent fasting protocol in order to achieve results. Most importantly, make sure you have a goal you'd like to achieve at the beginning of your fasting period. While at it remember that unlike many weight loss diets, fasting doesn't have a standard duration because it's just about depriving your body food for a given time.

Intermittent fasting is nothing curious or queer rather; it's part of normal everyday life. It's the most powerful and oldest intervention you can think of, yet so many people are not aware of its power to rejuvenate the body as well as its therapeutic potential. You don't have to put pressure on yourself to produce results in the beginning, especially if your goal is to lose weight. Take time to transition, allowing your body to adjust accordingly. This may mean starting with a plan that is close to your current eating plan, slowly advancing to intermittent eating plans that require you to fast for longer durations.

Chapter 6: Intermittent Fasting: The Best Anti-Aging Diet

Countless celebrities and entrepreneurs use intermittent fasting to reverses the effects of aging. However, not everyone understands the scientific aspect of intermittent fasting and its link with anti-aging. This chapter looks into the scientific aspect of intermittent fasting while introducing concepts related to aging healthily. To understand the relationship between fasting and anti-aging, you first need to understand the difference between the various fasting methods. For starters, the short-term fasting plans with a fasting window of between 16 and 20 hours offer multiple independent benefits. These fasts that are also known as micro-fasts support metabolic healthy by controlling body weight, lowering your insulin levels, and improving glycemic control. As such, short term fasting is an incredible choice to embrace when your goal is solely weight loss. During short fasts, your fat mass may reduce while physical strength remains the same.

The other benefits of fasting include an increase in brain-derived neurotrophic factor (BDNF) signaling within your brain, cardiovascular support, and reduced risk of cancer recurrence. On the other hand, fasting for extended periods will stimulate physiological changes that offer unique benefits of fasting that fall within functional areas like longevity, immune strength, and healthy aging.

The physiological effects of extended fasting are more pronounced than the effects of short-term fasts lasting less than 24 hours because of the body's ability to switch to fat and ketone catabolism upon the depletion of glycogen reserves during extended fasting. Extended fasting also increased the white blood cells that are a biomarker for immune health and is useful for adjunct therapy alongside chemotherapy for killing cancer cells. The rationale behind this is that cancer cells grow and thrive on glucose; thus, when you go on extended fasts; you starve the cancer cells and support the anti-cancer immune efforts.

Anti-Aging Benefits of Intermitted Fasting

Out of all interventions that are aimed at countering aging, calorie restriction is that most efficient. Generally, fasting for extended periods results in calorie restriction that reduces calories by between 20 and 40%. This is not recommended for performance and is unpopular among biohackers owing to mental distraction. Calorie restriction promotes five mechanisms that are essential for healthy aging. The following are mechanisms of extended fasting that promote healthy aging.

These processes are:

Cell proliferation (IGF-1 and TOR; specifically mTOR): Cell proliferation promotes balanced cell growth. It is the ability of the human system to be in the anabolic state with the presence of calories. That is, whenever calories are abundant, cells are in an anabolic state. When you're intermittent fasting results in caloric restriction that tends to shift the balance in the system through stimulation of catabolic pathways. The two pathways that are important in this process are the mammalian target of rapamycin (mTOR) and insulin-like growth factor-1 (IGF-1). Both IGF-1 and mTOR are nutrient sensors that regulate the cellular resources depending on the availability of calories. When you fast, fewer calories are leading to the down-regulation of mTOR and IGF-1, thus signaling repurposing and recycling of organelles and cells. A decline in mTOR signaling has been found to lead to lifespan extension.

Moreover, its inhibition is known to be a longevity assurance mechanism with the availability of rapamycin as well as other mTOR inhibitors making this pathway a valuable target for interventions that extend lifespan. Dr. Jason Fung, a proponent of intermittent fasting, agrees that mTOR is a protein sensor. He further says that eating fats alone and no protein can theoretically modulate MTOR positively. Thus, you can include fat-based drinks in your micro-fast.

Decreased Inflammation (NF-kB): The human body is bound to experience cumulative damage as you age. The damage is often identified by the immune receptors, thereby stimulating the production of multiple proinflammatory molecules. In the worst-case scenario, the accumulated damage is so extensive that the inflammation becomes continuous that either accompanies numerous age-related diseases or contributes to them. Inflammation on its own is not necessarily bad since its part of healing. However, evidence suggests that chronic inflammation and specifically age-associated inflammation, also referred to inflaming, heavily correlates with poor health biomarkers. Calorie restriction during intermittent fasting will inhibit nuclear factor kB (NF-kB) that exerts the anti-inflammatory effect. NF-kB is believed to the master regulator of inflammation, thus minimizing its activity will downregulate various parts of the proinflammatory signaling. Animal models suggest that this anti-inflammatory effect may have cognitive enhancing properties. One study focused on fasting as eustress; a form of stress that is beneficial versus distress; the negative stressors of life that speed up aging. The conclusion was that intermittent fasting led to a reduction of the plasma inflammatory factors. Thus, intermittent fasting can improve cognitive function and preserve the brain from distress through regulation of inflammatory response pathway. By engaging in intermittent fasting, you're able to attain the beneficial levels of stress that is necessary for your physiology and psychology.

Improved mitochondrial physiology (AMPK/SIRT): Mitochondria are the organelles that make up a cell. They're crucial in the production of cellular energy that enables the cells to do more work. This work is equivalent to physical labor, as is the case with the muscle cells or cognitive tasks in the case of brain cells. Aging tends to weaken the general quality of your body's mitochondrial network, thereby decreasing the destruction of already damaged or dysfunctional mitochondria as well as the generation of new mitochondria. However, when you fast and experience calorie restriction, these processes will be supported, giving rise to a high quality of your mitochondrial network. The two pathways that are mostly associated with mitochondrial support are sirtuins (SIRT genes) and AMP-dependent kinase (AMPK). Both pathways are sensitive to the shifts in the NADH/NAD+ ratio. Calorie restriction triggers an increase in NAD+ accumulation that activates sirtuins and AMPK. Studies have concluded that the fact that sirtuins need NAD for their enzymatic activity links metabolism to diseases associated with aging and aging. Both sirtuins and AMPK are central to mitochondrial biogenesis as well as processes of mitophagy (mitochondrial removing and recycling of the organelles that are dysfunctional that are associated with age) are important in maintaining a younger mitochondrial network. When cells are deprived of glucose during an extended fast, the production of ATP initially drops. When AMPK senses the decrease in ATP, it limits the utilization of energy as it upregulates numerous other processes that replenish ATP. As a result, mitochondria and cells are able to better make ATP in the future. Calorie restriction activates the AMPK pathway in a number of tissues in animal models. However, this has not been studied in humans.

Sirtuins also play an important role in aging as a biological stress sensor. Increasing and manipulating the expression of sirtuins in yeast promotes longevity.

Enhanced autophagy (FoxO): Autophagy can loosely be translated to self-eating. That is a cleaning mechanism that involves removal of organelles, old cell membranes as well as other cellular junk that has accumulated with time and is an impediment to optimal cellular performance. When the old and broken parts of your cells are removed, the growth hormone that is usually amplified during fasting will signal the body to start the production of new replacements. The result of autophagy is the renovation and recycling process of cells. mTOR will induce the activation of the forkhead box proteins. Both mitophagy and autophagy are FoxO-dependent suggesting that the transcriptional molecule is an integral component of the processes.

Increased antioxidant defenses (Nrf2): As humans age, there's an increase in the reactive oxygen species (ROS) while the natural antioxidant defenses decrease. Over time, this imbalance becomes greater even as the damage accumulates while the mitochondrial dysfunction becomes more prevalent. The normal production of oxidants in specific types of cells is important in the regulation of pathways (ROS are involved in some of the signaling processes). Therefore, it is valuable to strike the right balance as we age. This balance is may be critical for the optimization of mitochondrial performance and is referred to as mitohormesis with the idea being the need for the right amount of ROS with too little resulting in subpar performance while high amounts of ROS cause damage. This is important for those tissues that rely on the production of large amounts of ATP for metabolism such as heart, brain, and muscle. Among the understandings from mitorhormesis is that a certain amount of ROS is required to trigger adaptive responses that upregulate the antioxidant defenses as well as make mitochondria and cells better in dealing with toxins and stress. Thus, intermittent fasting can help in promoting anti-oxidant defenses. Calorie restriction will activate the nuclear factor (erythroid-derived 2) like 2 (Nfr2) that is a regulator of the cellular resistance to the oxidants. This protein plays a role in supporting antioxidant defenses through:

- Catabolism of peroxides and superoxide; eliminating all the bad stuff.
- Regeneration of oxidized proteins and cofactors (regrowing more of the good old stuff)
- Increase of redox transport (increasing efficiency of existing machinery)
- Synthesis of reducing factors (Creation of new good stuff)

Overall, Nrf2 is not the only mechanisms that promote antioxidant support and defenses. All the five mechanisms that are interrelated owing to the complex nature of human systems contribute to healthspan longevity. Like it is with all these other mechanisms, they support each other. For instance, mTOR is not only categorized under cell proliferation and autophagy.

Intermittent Fasting for Lifespan and Healthspan

Lifespan refers to the duration of time that you've lived. On the other hand, the duration within which you've been functional and healthy, and not just being alive is referred to as the healthspan. Calorie restriction that is initiated by any form of intermittent fasting is important in affecting both your lifespan and healthspan. It's not unusual to focus on the lifespan within the longevity and aging space at the expense of the quality of life you're living.

On the contrary, the duration of time you're functional and healthy is correlated with a higher quality of life. Your healthspan can be mediated by many things among them; dietary interventions, social interactions, exercise, family, and community. Social interaction is positively related to life satisfaction and longevity. Thus, healthspan it may be more valuable to emphasize lifespan alone.

Damage Accumulation vs. Programmed Aging

The debate between the importance of damage accumulation and programmed aging is unending. Humans are complex systems that involve a combination of both. Damage accumulation is characterized by mitochondrial and cellular damage, both of which happen at the cellular level with each amplifying the effects of the other. That is the changes in gene expression speed up damage accumulation, which in turn affects the ability of the cell to have healthy gene expression. On the other hand, programmed aging refers to changes in the manner in which our genes are expressed as we age. Some of the genes are underexpressed, while others are overexpressed.

Aging Benefits of Intermittent Fasting

The scientific aspect of the mechanisms that are involved in promoting longevity and aging go beyond the context of fasting. These mechanisms determine nootropics as well as the other techniques that we can use in supporting healthy aging. Although there are many benefits that arise when a certain degree of temporary starvation is induced, it's important to note that there are more ways to trigger these responses. Most importantly, you need to keep in mind that while some of the benefits will occur while you're in the fasted state, others will happen when you start eating normally. Thus, starvation primes the systems for rejuvenation even though it is refeeding that is credited for rebuilding new organelles and cells, thus increasing health.

Intermittent Fasting and Anti-aging Compounds

Excessive levels of pyrimidine and purine are signs that your body might be experiencing an increase in the levels of certain antioxidants. Specifically, researchers have found significant increases in carnosine and ergothioneine. A study on the individual variability in human blood metabolites found that the number of metabolites decreases as you age. These metabolites include ophthalmic acid, isoleucine, and leucine. This study also found that fasting significantly boosted the three metabolites and concluded that this explains how fasting extends the lifespan in rats. It is believed that the hike in antioxidants may be a survival response because when in the fasted state, the body experiences extreme levels of oxidative stress. Thus, the production of antioxidants can help in avoiding the potential damage that is a result of free radicals.

Intermittent Fasting and the Anti-Aging Molecule

Research has found that being in the fasted state is instrumental in triggering a molecule that can cause a delay in the aging of arteries. This is important in the prevention of chronic diseases that are age-related like cardiovascular disease, cancer, and Alzheimer's and is evidence that aging can be reversed. Vascular aging is the most important aspect of aging. Thus, when people grow older, they vessels supplying blood to various organs become more sensitive and more likely to experience aging damage; thus studying is vascular aging is important. According to the research done on starving mice generated a molecule known as beta-hydroxybutyrate that prevented vascular aging. This molecule is also a ketone that is produced by the liver and is handy as an energy source; then the glucose level is low. Ketones are mostly produced during starvation or fasting or when you're on a diet comprising low carbs and after a prolonged exercise. This molecule also promotes the multiplication and division of cells lining the blood vessels. This is a market of cellular youth.

Additionally, this compound is also able to delay vascular aging through endothelial cells that line lymphatic vessels and blood vessels. This can prevent the kind of cell aging that is referred to as cellular aging or senescence. Cellular senescence is defined as the irreversible cell cycle while at the same time preserving the cellular viability. Cellular senescence is suggested to work as a tumor suppressor mechanism as well as tissue remodeling promoter after wounding. These cells show marked changes in morphology that includes irregular shape size, enlarged size, multiple and prominent nuclei, increased granularity, accumulation of lysosomal, and mitochondrial mass.

Chapter 7: The Golden Key: Autophagy

The cells in the human body are constantly being damaged as metabolic processes take place hence the need for autophagy to clear these damaged cells. The word autophagy comes from two Greek words; 'auto' which means self and 'phagy' meaning eating. Thus, autophagy is the process where the body consumes its own tissue in the wake of metabolic processes that occur due to certain diseases and starvation. Researchers consider autophagy to be a survival mechanism or the body's clever way of responding to stress to protect itself.

When you think of it as a form of self-eating, it's definitely scary. So is autophagy good for your health? Definitely! This is the body's normal way of initiating the process of cellular renewal. Autophagy may seem like a relatively new concept, yet our bodies have been using it for millions of years. The first autophagy studies were conducted on yeast with the progress of this study leading to a Nobel Prize in

Physiology or Medicine for Dr. Yoshinori Ohsumi, a Japanese scientist for his discoveries of the mechanisms of autophagy in October 2016. According to the study, the body can eliminate all the clutter within whenever it feels the need to conserve the energy for other most important purposes. The cleaning mechanism of autophagy is critical in the elimination of just about every kind of toxins, misfolded proteins, germs, bacteria, and pathogens. So beneficial is autophagy that is key in preventing diseases like liver disease, cancer, infections, diabetes, cardiomyopathy, neurodegeneration, autoimmune diseases. Autophagy offers multiple anti-aging benefits by helping in destroying and reusing damaged components that occur within cells. Thus, this process uses the waste generated within cells to create new building materials that facilitate regeneration and repair. Although the process of autophagy doesn't require any outside help, you'll definitely begin feeling more relaxed and energetic once it takes place.

While recent studies have revealed the role of autophagy in cleaning and defending the body from the negative effects of stress, the exact way autophagy processes work is just beginning to be understood. Several processes are involved. For instance, lysosomes form part of the cells that are capable of destroying large damages cells such as mitochondria as well as help in transporting the damaged parts, so they are used to generate fuel. To sum it up, the damaged material must be transported by a lysosome, before it's deconstructed and spit back out for repurposing.

Essential Autophagy Steps

The process of autophagy involves the following steps as follows:

1. Creation of phagophore by a protein kinase complex as well as a lipid kinase complex. These two work together in sourcing a membrane that will eventually become the phagophore.

2. Once the phagophore is formed, the next step is its expansion. In this stage, a protein that is known as LC3 is bonded with the just formed phogophore through multiple autophagy-related proteins that are referred to as the ATG. When the bonding of the two is complete, the LC3 protein then becomes LC3-II. This formation occurs around cytoplasm material, which is then due to be degraded. This material may be random or selected specifically if it includes misfolded proteins and damaged organelles. When the process of replacement begins, ATG-9, a transmembrane protein acting as a protector of the site of phagophore formation is formed. This protein is assumed to help in expansion by increasing the number of phagophore membrane by supplying them from adjacent membrane locations.

3. The phagophore undergoes changes in its shape becoming elongated and closing, thereby becoming an autophagosome. The autophagosome serves as a holder of materials that are then degraded.

4. Both lysosome and autophagosome membranes fuse together. The lysosomal lumen (space within a lysosome) have hydrolases. Hydrolases break down molecules into smaller pieces using water to demolish the chemical bonds. When the lysosome and autophagosome fuse together, an exposure of the material that is inside the autophagosome to chemical wrecking balls occurs. The fusion converts the lysosome into an autolysosome.

5. The hydrolases degrade all material found within the autophagosome together with the inner membrane. The macromolecules that are the result of this process are waddled around by permeases that are on the autolysosome membrane until they get back to their original cytoplasm. At this point, the cell may reuse the macromolecules.

Well, this is how autophagy works. It's a complex yet important process that is still being studied to ensure further understanding.

There are different kinds of autophagy that include micro and macroautophagy as well as chaperone-mediated autophagy. Macroautophagy is the most popular of the three. It is an evolutionarily conserved anabolic process that involves the formation of autophagosomes (vesicles) that surround cellular organelles and macromolecules. Apart from humans' mold, yeast, flies, worms, and mammals also benefit from autophagy.

Macroautophagy is the process where catalyzation of non-functional cellular constituents to lysosome of cells takes place. What this process does is a separation of the cytoplasm of cells that includes different cell organs, degrading them to amino acids.

Inducing Autophagy With Intermittent Fasting

One of the common questions about autophagy is when does it occur? Generally, autophagy is usually active in all the cells. However, there's increased response to acute energy shortage, nutrient deprivation, and stress. This means that you can cause your body to go into autophagy using good stressors such as temporary calorie restriction and exercise. These have been linked with longevity, weight control as well as inhibiting a number of age-related diseases.

You can induce autophagy through intermittent fasting. When you restrain yourself from eating food for a while, it will eventually trigger autophagy. When you fast for long, your body will start feeling deprived of supply hence can begin catabolic processes at the macromolecular level. This means identifying those processes that are misusing the available energy like parasites, pathogens, mold, fungi, and bacteria within that don't give back anything for elimination. Once your body goes into autophagy, it begins the elimination by identifying all misfolded proteins and recycling them to produce energy and new cells. Not only does this process clean your body but also promote restrengthening. The body also identifies chronic inflammations, disorders, and diseases that make us ill and use the energy of the body and eliminates them. When the elimination begins, even chronic inflammations that have troubled you for years will go away, making autophagy a powerful mechanism of treatment. This also has a powerful anti-aging effect because it stops those processes that hasten the signs of aging. Autophagy also has a great impact on the cognitive function in addition to stopping neurodegenerative disorders and reversing their effects. This means that disorders like Parkinson's and Alzheimer's can be brought under control. Autophagy also promotes cardiovascular health, lowers immunity problems, hypertension, and chronic inflammation. This process is guaranteed to give you a boon for a rejuvenated life.

Studies suggest that the autophagy process starts anywhere between 24 and 48 hours after your last meal. This is perhaps one of the best ways of inducing autophagy. Therefore, if you would like to trigger autophagy, then you must fast for longer. Alternate day fasting and water fasting are the most ideal. If you opt for alternate day fasting, make sure that you don't eat anything during the 36-hour fasting window. Don't consume any calories from soft drinks or juices either. On the other hand, if you go for the water fast, you must do it for 2 to 3 days as your recommended fasting window of between 24 to 48 hours.

Ultimately, the best intermittent fasting you can employ to induce autophagy is alternate day fast without consuming any calories in the fasting window. If you feel you're up to it, you can take it a notch higher with a 2- t0 3-day water fast once in three months. Looking at the benefits, it's definitely worth restraining yourself from eating to get your body into autophagy.

Exercise is another source of good stress that has been found to induce autophagy. According to recent research, exercise induces autophagy in a number of organs that take part in metabolic regulation like liver, muscle, adipose tissue, and pancreas. Although exercise has many benefits to the body, it's a form of stress since it breaks down tissues and causes them to be repaired so that they grow back stronger. Although the extent of exercise required to boost autophagy is not clear, research suggests that going into intense exercise is most beneficial. If you want to combine fasting and exercise, then you must approach it with caution. You just might be surprised that you actually feel energetic once you get the hang of fasting.

Apart from fasting and exercise, there are certain foods which, when eaten, will contribute towards inducing autophagy. Generally speaking, you need to focus on low carb foods, some of which include the following:

Herbs and spices such as cayenne pepper, black pepper, ginseng, ginger, cinnamon, turmeric, cumin, cardamom, parsley, thyme, cilantro, coriander, rosemary, and basil.

Berries and other fruits; strawberries, raspberries, blueberries, elderberries, cherries and cranberries.

Drinks; tea and coffee. Your coffee and tea should have no cream, milk, or sugar. As such, it's better to go for herbal, green, or black tea. Avoid fruit tea since it's too sweet. You may also have distilled vinegar or apple cider.

Alcoholic drinks; vodka, vermouth, gin, whiter, and red wine.

You could also try foods that are healthy for your body that include the following:

Fruits such as; olive, avocado, coconut, watermelon, cantaloupe, and honeydew.

Veggies; squash, tomato, peas, spinach, bell pepper, pickles, beetroot, green beans, carrots, and turnip.

Seeds and nuts; brazil nuts, almonds, cashews, chia seeds, chestnuts, flax seeds, macadamia, hazelnuts, pecans, peanuts, pistachios, pine nuts, pumpkin seeds, sunflower, sesame seeds, walnuts, peanut butter, almond butter, cashew butter, and macadamia nut butter.

Dairy and milk; blue cheese, buttermilk, brie cheese, Colby cheese, cheddar cheese, cottage cheese, cream cheese, Monterey jack cheese, mozzarella, feta cheese, swiss cheese, parmesan, mascarpone, sour cream, heavy cream, skimmed milk, and whole milk.

Fats; coconut milk, coconut cream, red palm oil, olive oil, MCT oil, macadamia oil, flaxseed oil, coconut oil, cocoa butter, avocado oil, beef tallow, lard, lard, ghee and butter.

Protein shakes with water; whey protein shake, hemp protein shake, rice protein shake, pea protein shake, and microgreens blend.

Drinks; almond water, almond milk, coconut water, kombucha, and coconut milk.

Alcoholic drinks; cognac, tequila, champagne, beer, mint liquor and chocolate liquor.

There's more to learn about autophagy and the best way of inducing it. Combing fasting and regular exercise as part of your daily routine is a great place to start. If you're taking certain medications for any health condition, you must consult your doctor before you go into fasting.

Uses of Autophagy

The main function of autophagy is degrading and breaking down organelles in cells. This process contributes to the repair of cells. Autophagy also acts as part of the body's repair mechanism. Autophagy also plays an important role in a number of cellular functions like yeast the high levels of autophagy are activated by nutrient starvation. In addition to degrading unnecessary proteins, autophagy is also helpful in recycling amino acids that in turn, are important in synthesizing proteins that are crucial for survival. In the case of animals, they experience nutrient depletion after birth due to severing transplacental food supply. It is at this point that autophagy is activates helping to mediate the nutrient depletion. Another function of autophagy is xenophagy, which is the breaking down of the infectious particles.

Benefits of Autophagy

Although autophagy presents multiple benefits, there are two major benefits of this process:

Autophagy eliminates waste cells, misfolded proteins, and pathogens from your body. Autophagy is instrumental in ridding the body of all waste that is making you sick and contributing to inefficient functioning. It removes the pathogens that live inside your body, thriving on your energy and making you experience good health. The presence of wasted cells and misfolded proteins often clutter your body. Autophagy comes in to recycle and clean them up, giving your body new cells while also releasing energy that your body can use when there's an extreme shortage.

Autophagy helps to improve muscle performance. When you exercise, the stress on your cells causes energy to go up, making parts get worn out faster. Autophagy, therefore, helps in removing the damage and keeping the energy needs in check.

Autophagy helps in the prevention of neurodegenerative disorders. Most of the neurodegenerative disorders are a result of damaged proteins forming around neurons. Thus, autophagy offers protection by eliminating these proteins. In particular, autophagy will help clear proteins associated with Alzheimer's, Parkinson's, and Huntington's diseases.

Autophagy enhances metabolic efficiency. Autophagy can be activated to help in improving the work of mitochondria the smallest part of the cell. This makes the cells work efficiently hence becoming more efficient.

Autophagy slows down the progression of certain diseases. Diseases too need energy for them to spread in the body. Thus, by starving them of energy, they're unable to function. For instance, cancer cells usually function like the normal body cells thriving on glucose obtained through food. When you go on a fast and deprive the body of this energy, the progression of cancer stops dramatically since they can't rely on fat energy to spread. In the same way, when you live on a fat diet, your body will begin burning fat hence literally starving cancer. This also applies to other chronic inflammations that flourish in your body silently because of the availability of energy that will begin to go when you're on extended fasts.

Autophagy helps fight against infectious diseases. Autophagy removes toxins that cause infections in addition to helping your body improve the way your body responds to infections. Most importantly, viruses and intracellular bacteria can be removed by autophagy.

Common Misconceptions About Autophagy

Intermittent fasting has become popular over the years, effectively shifting the spotlight on autophagy. As a result, many people have come up with speculations and assumptions about autophagy that are untrue. Here are some of the false beliefs about people hold autophagy:

You can trigger autophagy with a 24-hour fast. Neither will a 16-hour or 24-hour fast trigger autophagy. This is because this is such a short time frame. Instead, if you want to trigger autophagy within a short time, then high-intensity exercise is recommended. The reason autophagy can't happen after a 24-hour fast is simple. Fasting doesn't happen soon after your last meal because then your body has to digest the food and draw energy from it. Thus, after your last fast, the body will be in a postabsorptive state of metabolism for a couple of hours. Remember, it takes more time to digest certain foods. Foods like fibers, vegetables, fat, and protein don't digest that easy. Because of this, the body will not be getting into the fasted state until after a period of 5 to 6 hours of going without food. The reason is simple. Before that, you're still in a fed state as your body thrives on the calories you've consumed. For example, if you had your last meal at 7pm, it will not be until midnight when you actually begin the actual physiological fast. Therefore, while you'll claim to be going on a 16- to 20-hour fast, in reality, you've spent about 12 hours fasting. This is such a short time to trigger autophagy. Even then, your fast is not in vain because you'll still experience the other benefits of intermittent fasting that include; low inflammation levels, reduced insulin levels, and fat burning.

More is better. You need a minimum of three days fasting to experience autophagy. That is by the time you're getting to your third day of fasting; you'll enjoy benefits of autophagy and fasting as this will energize your body to fight off tumors, cancer cells as well as boost the production of stem cells. Even then, prolonged autophagy is not the best. If anything, it can have side effects that include providing ample ground for the production of bacteria and Brucella. Extended autophagy may also see the resilience of tumor cells because they're strengthened, thus becoming more resistant to treatment. The essential autophagy gene ATG6/BECN1 that encodes Beclin 1 protein and is vital in reducing cancer cells may instead feed the cancer cells, thus giving them the strength they need to survive. Finally, there's a risk of muscle wasting and sarcopenia that affects longevity. Although you can't dispute the fact that autophagy is incredible, you need to be aware that it's not good to always be in this state. Otherwise, you'll end up with unwanted repercussions as well as health hazards. Thus, it's best to induce autophagy intermittently; don't make it a constant process.

Autophagy means starvation. Some people believe that autophagy will make you starve. This is untrue. Although you have to avoid eating for an extended period to achieve autophagy, this is totally different from starvation. Staying away from food for a couple of days will not make you starve because people who are starving don't even have the energy to go about their lives and daily activities like someone who is practicing intermittent fasting will. Intermittent fasting doesn't deprive your body of energy since the body stores unused energy as fats that it resorts to whenever there's scarcity. This is not only in overweight and obese people but also those with a lean mass.

Additionally, autophagy breaks down misfolded proteins and old cells that serve as additional sources of energy when you are not feasting. Thus, your body turns to other body components for energy. After a couple of days of fasting, you get to experience ketosis where your normal metabolism is suspended due to the absence of new food consumption. Thus, the body begins to use ketones and stored fats to draw energy for the muscle and brain. You eventually get to improve your lifespan through basal autophagy.

Autophagy makes you build muscle. This is an outright lie because you need calories to build muscles. Therefore, building muscles during autophagy will be close to impossible since there's no additional source of energy when you're staying away from food. Moreover, proteins are essential to muscle building are it requires a vital process that is referred to as protein synthesis. Intermittent fasting limits your protein intake is limited; thus, your body easily switches to a catabolic state where it breaks down as opposed to an anabolic state where it grows. Remember, autophagy can still breakdown old protein floating around your body cells that are central to muscle protein synthesis. However, experts point to the fact that with proper meal choice, you can maintain your muscle mass during intermittent fasting.

Coffee hinders autophagy. Taking coffee doesn't have any impact on your body's ability to achieve autophagy. In fact, taking coffee is good for inducing autophagy and ketosis because coffee contains polyphenols, that is a compound that promotes autophagy. Thus, coffee supports the process of autophagy. Caffeine also contributes to the body enjoying lipolysis that burns fat while reducing insulin, thus improving ketones and boosting AMPK. Although it doesn't hinder autophagy, you shouldn't take your coffee with sugar, sweeteners or even cream as these can increase the insulin level, thus stopping any benefit, you'd get from fasting.

When you exercise, you stop autophagy. Exercising is among the proven ways of inducing autophagy. Simply put, activity triggers autophagy. Resistance training is an excellent way of increasing mTOR signaling. While exercising will not activate mTOR in the same manner that eating does, exercise will translocate mTOR complex near the cellular membrane, preparing it for action as soon as you begin eating. By working out, you become more sensitive to activating mTOR; this will trigger more growth after working out. In addition, you also get to activate autophagy with in-depth resistance training that can help in reducing the breakdown and destruction of muscles by regulating the IGF-1 as well as its receptors. Apart from fasting, the other best approach to increasing autophagy is working out. Ultimately, you can combine both in order to attain the best results.

Eating fruits will not stop autophagy. Most of the fruits are laden with fructose that is digested by the liver before being stored as liver glycogen. When you have excess levels of fructose, it's converted to triglycerides. Thus, eating fruits will definitely work against ketosis and autophagy as it promotes liver glycogen storage. The content of glycogen in the liver makes sure that there's a balance between the mTOR and AMPK. When you consume fruits with a regulated amount of fats and protein may help in remaining in a catabolic state of breaking down molecules. Even then, the chance of experiencing autophagy is quite slim.

Most of the autophagy research has been done on yeast and rats. Genetic screening studies have found at least 32 different autophagy-related genes. Research continues to show the importance of autophagic processes as a response to stress and starvation. As you may know, insulin is the hormone that is responsible for letting glucose in the blood to enter the cells, thus energizing them for proper functioning. Thus, the more glucose you ingest, the more likely it will be stored in the blood effectively raising your insulin levels and blood sugar. Even then, the insulin will only get active and begins working if magic when its level decreases, thereby regulating your blood level. It's important to understand that fasting for extended periods is not easy; hence, you'll do well to start with intermittent fasting, which, when done on a regular basis produces the benefits of autophagy.

Chapter 8: The Seven Types of Intermittent Fasting Diets

Intermittent fasting is about changing your pattern of eating. You can choose to abstain from eating partially or entirely for a specified period before you can begin eating again. As such, there are many different methods of fasting. These methods vary in terms of the number of days, hours, and calorie allowances. With intermittent fasting, every person's lifestyle and experience is unique; hence, different styles will suit different people. Here are 7 common types of intermittent fasting diets:

The 12:12 Diet

With this diet, you need to adhere to a 12-hour fasting window and a subsequent 12-hour feeding window every day. This means that if you eat dinner at 9 p.m., you won't have breakfast until 9 a.m. the following morning. This intermittent fasting protocol is perhaps the easiest to follow. This plan is particularly good for beginners because of the relatively small fasting window. You can also opt to incorporate sleep in the fasting window, which means you'll be asleep for most of the fasting window. Apart from helping you lose fat and weight, this plan offers numerous benefits. First, it helps you break from the habit of binge eating or snacking at midnight mindlessly. Secondly, it helps in clearing inflammation as well as getting rid of damaged cells, thereby preventing cancer while also promoting healthy gut microbes. Fasting at night stimulates cell regeneration that has a positive effect on cancer, dementia, heart attacks, and dementia.

When you go for the 12:12 fasting plan, caution must be taken when choosing food so that you only take low-fat food with high protein and low carbohydrates. Most importantly, stay away from processed food. When followed to the latter, the 12:12 plan yields incredible results that include improved brain health, reduced inflammation, enhanced detoxification, and weight loss. To incorporate the 12:12 plan in your day, make sure that you leave 12 hours between your evening and morning meal. You can, however, take water and unsweetened tea.

16:8 Intermittent Fasting Plan

The 16:8 intermittent fasting plan limits your consumption of foods and beverages containing calories to 8 hours a day while abstaining from eating for the remainder of the 16 hours. You can repeat this cycle frequently from once to twice a day or even make it your daily routine depending on what you prefer. This plan is common among those looking to burn fat and lose weight. There are no strict regulations and rules, making it easy to follow and see the result with so little effort. It's also flexible and less restrictive hence can fit into just about any lifestyle. Apart from weight loss, the 16:8 will also help to improve blood sugar control, enhanced longevity, and boost brain function.

Getting Started With 16:8

The 16:8 plan is safe, simple, and sustainable. To begin, you need to pick an appropriate eating window within which you limit your food intake. Most people prefer eating between noon and 8 p.m. so that they skip breakfast. You may also have your eating window between 9 a.m. and 5 p.m. allowing you plenty of time for healthy breakfast, a normal lunch and a light dinner or snack. Since everyone is different, you can experiment with different timings and see what works for your lifestyle and schedule. Regardless of what you choose to eat, make sure you space out to have several small meals and snacks throughout the day. This is important in stabilizing your blood sugar levels and keeping hunger under control. To maximize the potential of health benefits, make sure you're only consuming nutritious whole beverages and foods during your eating.

Having nutrient-rich foods helps in rounding out your diet so that you reap the rewards of this eating plan. While at it, make sure you're drinking calorie-free beverages such as water and unsweetened coffee and tea to keep your appetite in check. The 16:8 plan is easy to follow since it cuts down the time you spend preparing food and cooking every week. Some of the benefits associated with this plan include improved blood sugar control, increased weight loss, and enhanced longevity. On the flipside, this plan also has drawbacks. Restricting your food consumption to eight hours can cause you to eat more during the eating window in a bid to make up for the time spent fasting. This can lead to weight gain, development of unhealthy eating habits, and digestive weight gain. You may also experience some short-term negative side effects like weakness, fatigue, and hunger when starting out. Some research findings suggest that intermittent fasting affects women differently and could interfere with reproduction and fertility. Therefore, make sure you consult your doctor before you start.

5:2 Intermittent Fasting Plan

The 5:2 intermittent fasting plan is also referred to as The Fast Diet. This plan, which was popularized by British journalist Michael Mosley, lets you have five days of normal eating and two days of restricted calories to a quarter of your daily needs, usually 500-600 per day. The plan doesn't spell out the specific days you should eat or fast. You're at liberty to make this decision. For instance, you can decide to fast on Mondays and Thursdays where you eat two to three small meals and eat normally for the rest of the days. Even then, you need to know that eating normally doesn't imply eating anything, including junk or even binge eating because then you won't lose weight but instead gain.

A study on the 5:2 diet found that this diet has the potential of causing weight loss that is similar to regular restriction of calories. This plan was also effective in the reduction of insulin levels as well as improving insulin sensitivity.

The 5:2 plan can be effective when done in the right manner because it lets you consume fewer calories. Thus, you shouldn't compensate for the fasting days by eating more than you'd normally eat when you're not fasting. There's no rule on when and what you should eat on the days when you're fasting. One of the side effects you'll experience at that beginning of this program is extreme episodes of hunger accompanied by feelings of weakness and sluggish. However, this tends to fade with time, especially when you're busy with other things. Eventually, they find it easier to fast. Should you notice that you're repeatedly feeling unwell or faint, be sure to talk to your doctor. The 5:2 plan, just like any other plan is not suitable for everyone. Some of the people who should avoid this plan include people who experience drops in blood sugar levels, people with an eating disorder, and people who are malnourished and underweight with known nutrient deficiencies.

Alternate Day Intermittent Fasting

With this plan, you fast on one day and eat the next day. This means that you're restricting what you'll be eating half the time. When you're fasting, you can drink calorie-free beverages like unsweetened tea, coffee, and water. Studies on alternate day fasting reveal that you can lose 3-8% of your body weight between 2 and 12 weeks. You can also consider modified alternate fasting that lets you have 500 calories on fasting days and is more tolerable because of the decreased amounts of hunger hormones and an increase in the satiety hormones. Alternate day fasting will not only help you to lose weight but also help in lowering insulin levels in type 2 diabetes patients. Type 2 diabetes makes up 90-95% of diabetes cases in the US.

Moreover, more than two-thirds of Americans are considered to be pre-diabetic, which means they've higher blood sugar levels that can't be categorized as diabetes. Restricting calories and losing weight is an effective means of improving or reversing the symptoms of type 2 diabetes. Alternate day fasting also contributes to mild reductions in risk factors for type 2 diabetes in obese and overweight individuals.

Most importantly, alternate day fasting is especially effective in reducing insulin resistance and lowering insulin levels with a minor effect on blood sugar control. Excessive insulin levels have been linked to obesity, cancer, heart disease, and other chronic diseases. Thus, insulin resistance and a dip in insulin levels can lead to a significant decline in type 2 diabetes. Evidence suggests that alternate day fasting is a great option for weight loss and reducing risk factors for heart disease. Other common health benefits of alternate day fasting are:

- Decreased blood triglycerides
- Lower LDL cholesterol concentration
- Decreased blood pressure
- Reduced waist circumference
- Increased number of large LDL particles and reduction in dangerous small, dense LDL particles.

One of the common effects of alternate day fasting is its ability to stimulate autophagy. This gives you the added advantage of having parts of old cells degraded and recycled. This process is crucial in preventing diseases like cancer, neurodegeneration, cancer, and infections. In addition, it also contributes to delaying aging as well as reducing the risk of tumors.

Warrior Fasting Diet

The warrior diet was created by Ori Hofmekler, who was a former member of the Israeli Special Forces. This intermittent fasting plan is based on the eating patterns of ancient warriors that feasted at night and ate little during the day. This plan is designed to improve the way we feel, eat, look, and perform by stressing the body through reduced consumption of food hence triggering survival instincts. According to Ori Hofmekler, this diet is not based on science but on personal observations and beliefs. When you follow this diet, you're required to under eat for at least 20 hours a day, that is considered to be the fasting period but eat as much food at night. You should aim at eating small amounts of foods such as hard-boiled eggs, dairy products, vegetables and fruits, and non-caloric fluids. You then have a four-hour feeding window. It is recommended that you stick to healthy, organic, and unprocessed food choices. Like other intermittent fasting plans, warrior fasting helps you burn fat, boost your energy levels, improve concentration/brain health, decrease inflammation, control blood sugar, and stimulate cellular repair.

Despite all these health benefits that the warrior diet promises, it also has some potential downfalls that include the following:

It's inappropriate for most people. This diet is inappropriate for most people, including expectant women, children, extreme athletes, people with diseases such as type 1 diabetes, and underweight people.

It can be difficult to stick to for some people. This is an obvious limitation of this diet because it restricts the time that you can eat substantial meals to just four hours. This can be difficult to maintain, especially if you desire to go out for lunch or breakfast.

Warrior fasting can cause disordered eating. This plan emphasizes on overeating that can be problematic for most people. However, Ori argues that you should know when you're satisfied and stop eating.

It can result in negative side effects. Some of the negative side effects that the warrior diet can potentially cause some of which can be severe include dizziness, fatigue, anxiety, low energy, insomnia, lightheadedness, constipation, fainting, hormonal imbalance, irritability and weight gain among others. Additionally, health professionals hold the opinion that this fasting plan can result in nutrients deficiency. However, you can take care of this by making sure you're eating nutrient-dense food.

Unlike other intermittent fasting plans, the warrior fasting plan has three phases:

Phase 1 - Detox. Start by under eating for 20 hours daily. You can eat anything from the clear broth, vegetable juices, hard boiled eggs, raw fruits, and vegetables. In your four-hour eating window, include whole grains, plant proteins, cooked vegetables, salads, and cheese. You can also take water, small amounts of milk, tea, and coffee throughout the day. The whole idea is to detox.

Phase 2. This week, your focus should be on high fat. Therefore, you shouldn't consume any starches or grains but instead focus on eating foods like vegetable juices, dairy, clear broth, raw fruits, hard boiled eggs lean animal protein as well as cooked vegetables.

Phase 3. This is the phase where you conclude your fat loss. Thus, it cycles between periods of high protein and high carb intake. This would mean 1-2 days of high carbs, followed by 1-2 days of high protein and low cards.

Eat Stop Eat Intermittent Fasting

The Eat stop eat intermittent fasting regimen involves fasting for 24 hours once or twice weekly. This method was made popular by Brad Pilon, a fitness expert and has been quite popular over the past few years. You fast from dinner one day to dinner the next day amounting to 24 hours of being in the fasted state. This means that if you finish dinner at 8 p.m., you don't eat anything until 8 p.m. the next day to make a full 24-hour fast. This fasting plan is not restricted to dinner alone; you can also fast from breakfast to breakfast or better still lunch to lunch and get the same end result. Like other intermittent fasting plans, you can take coffee, water, and other beverages with zero calories during the fast. However, no solid food is allowed. If your goal of doing the 24-hour weekly fast is to lose weight, make sure you're eating normally during your eating period. That is, just consume the same amount of food you'd be normally consuming without keeping the fast in mind. The challenge with this 24-hour fast is that it's fairly difficult for many people because of the length of the fasting window. Thus, you don't have to go all the way at the beginning. You can begin with 14-16 hours of fasting, increasing the duration with time. Generally, the first few hours of the fast will be easy before you become ravenously hungry. However, with discipline and taking enough fluid during the fasting duration, you can be sure to pull through. Soon, you'll get used to doing these fasts.

Spontaneous Meal Skipping

You don't have to stick to a specific intermittent fasting plan to reap the benefits. You could actually consider meal skipping. You can opt to skip meals from time to time when you're too busy to cook, or you don't feel hungry. Skipping one or two meals whenever you feel inclined basically means you're doing a spontaneous intermittent fast. It is simple; you can skip your lunch and have an early dinner. Alternatively, if you eat a large dinner, you can skip breakfast instead. Skipping meals can boost your metabolism Skipping meals is a good place to start your intermittent fasting experience, especially if the idea of going for long periods without food intimidates you. This intermittent fasting plan bursts the myth that you need to eat after every few hours; otherwise, your body will get into starvation mode or even lose muscle. The truth is that the human body is equipped very well to handle extended periods of famine, let alone having to do without a meal or two from time to time. Therefore, if there's a day you're really not hungry, you can skip breakfast so that you have healthy lunch and dinner. This fast is also convenient if you're traveling somewhere but just can't find something you can eat. You just must sure that you eat healthy foods.

Chapter 9: Cautions While Making the Transition to Intermittent Fasting

Preparation is the key to succeeding in intermittent fasting. When you prepare well, you can be sure to stay in control so that you're not feeling lost and out of place. If you want to reap the benefits of intermittent fasting quickly, you must be keen to make the right move when getting into this practice. Your body is accustomed to eating after 2-3 hours; therefore, you need to immerse yourself into fasting systematically. Although this sounds simple in principle, it's actually not easy when you start out. However, when you take caution and come up with a good plan, you'll have a smooth transition that will contribute to the success of your intermittent fasting quest. Here are some cautions you can consider while making the transition to intermittent fasting:

Transition slowly. It's okay to be ambitious about going without food for several hours. However, as you're starting out, you need to be careful not to be too ambitious by immersing yourself into intermittent fasting that requires you to fast for extended periods. It's advisable to consider starting with the simpler intermittent fasting protocols and advance to the extended protocols over time. If anything, you gained the weight you're trying to shed off after a long time, so don't expect to lose weight overnight. For instance, you can start with the 12:12 intermittent fasting protocol where you have a fasting window of 12 hours to advancing on to 16:8 that lets you fast for 16 hours and eat for 8 hours. You can even take a break after a couple of days or weeks before attempting again. The trick is to make sure that you're adding on another day every week until you're able to stick to your intermittent fasting plan. Only then can you consider trying intermittent fasting protocols that require you to fast for extended periods of between 18 and 24 hours like 5:2 or warrior depending on how comfortable you're. Don't hesitate to tailor the fasting protocol to your preference, even if it means not doing it every day.

Take your schedule into account. It's very important to keep your schedule in mind while planning for the intermittent fasting protocol that's right for you. Your choice of an intermittent fasting protocol should not be influenced by peer pressure rather, by what is suitable for you in relation to your schedule. Don't go for an extreme plan in the beginning just because your friends are doing it. If there's no way you can have your meals within an 8-hour window because your schedule is erratic, then the LeanGains 16:8 protocol is not appropriate for you. However, if you are sure you can't go for 24 hours without food, then this intermittent plan might be the most suitable for you. Ultimately, you must think about your schedule, your preferences, and if the plan will affect the other people that you live with before deciding what is best for you. This will make your transition to intermittent fasting smooth.

Don't start intermittent fasting alongside a new diet. If your goal is to lose weight and you're also interested in taking on a new diet like low-calorie diet or keto, make sure you're not starting it alongside intermittent fasting. This is because it takes time for your body to adjust to the new meals and foods included in your diet. Moreover, whether you're cutting down on meat on your vegetarian diet or you're simply reducing your carbs dramatically, it will have a huge effect on your body when combined with intermittent fasting. Therefore, to succeed with intermittent fasting, make sure that you stick to your diet for up to two weeks before adding intermittent fasting. This way, you will have a great understanding of your body, hence a smooth transition.

Eliminate snacks. Snacks refer to anything that will add empty calories to your system and cause cravings. Before beginning intermittent fasting, make sure you prepare your body to stay without food for longer periods than usual. The first step towards this is eliminating snacks. Although not evident, snacks are your biggest enemies because they're not nutritious; rather, they're only full of salt, sugar, flours, and refined oil. Thus, you must learn to avoid them in order to stay in shape. Snacks often cause your blood sugar levels to spike while loading your system with empty calories and provide very little to your gut. Make sure you eliminate snacks from your routine. You also need to avoid carbonated beverages that add empty calories and are full of sugar.

Most importantly, keep in mind that intermittent fasting is not based on restricting your calorie intake so you can consume calories within a limit that is reasonable. Rather, your calorie intake will automatically reduce since your eating windows are short. Remember, intermittent fasting is based on when you eat and not what you eat. One of the best ways to avoid processed foods is staying away from foods that are served at fast food chains, including salads that have various dressings. Instead, make it a habit to cook your own food. This will ensure you're only eating healthy food.

Stay true to your purpose. There's definitely a reason why you're getting into intermittent fasting. Staying true to this reason is the only way you'll stay grounded to the cause. Therefore, make sure you have defined the reason why you're going into fasting. This may be losing weight; fasting will reduce the level of hormones like insulin while increasing the human growth hormone and norepinephrine that make the stored body fat more accessible hence making it possible for you to burn fat and effectively lose weight. Fasting also helps in the prevention of heart disease, diabetes, as well as reduce inflammation. Most importantly, fasting will also offer protection against cancer, Alzheimer's while increasing longevity.

Face your fears. It's normal to feel nervous and even harbor doubts before beginning intermittent fasting, especially because we have been cultured to believe that breakfast is the most important meal of the day. However, you need to know that when unaddressed these worries can cause you to stop. Therefore, face them. It's important to know that breakfast is a neutral meal hence can be skipped. In fact, the reality is that skipping breakfast will not make you gain weight while eating breakfast will not rave up your metabolism. You also need to keep in mind that fasting will increase your metabolic rate and help you lose weight while retaining more muscle.

Begin with 3 meals. Intermittent fasting is all about a total lifestyle change. Therefore, you need to start by taking three meals. This may be surprising, and you may be wondering whether the fact that you're already skipping a meal means you are doing intermittent fasting. Well, the answer is no. Here's why; while you don't have time to consume three meals on any given day, you somewhat take improper meals in the course of the day. This kind of munching counts for intermittent fasting. Thus, we must consider starting off with a balanced breakfast, eat moderate lunch, and finish with a light dinner. When you get to a point where you're able to sustain without difficulty with the three meals you'll be ready to move on to intermittent fasting.

Be consistent with your intermittent fasting protocol. It's likely that you will be excited to make a change and transition to the next intermittent fasting protocol after some time. This is especially the case when you begin seeing results. Even then, you must remember that intermittent fasting mustn't be rushed. Make sure you stay on a single fasting protocol for at least two weeks before moving on to the next. Keep in mind that each of the intermittent fasting protocols presents its own unique results and advantages. Only when you get comfortable should you consider moving on to the next one.

No fasting protocol is superior. It's a common misconception that you can only get better results when you go for the tougher regimen. While there's some degree of truth in this belief, it's important to focus on individual capacity. Everyone has their unique capabilities, thus imitating someone else is utterly meaningless. Some people may post impressive results with a 12-hour fasting protocol while for others, it will take another protocol to experience similar results. So don't go for the toughest protocol but instead find a protocol that suits you.

Focus on eating healthy eating. One of the things that you're likely to ignore when starting intermittent fasting is the quality of food you're eating. Although your fast will generally involve cutting down on the number of calories you're consuming, it's equally important to be deliberate about your food choices. More specifically, focus on healthy eating, especially if you're aiming to make this a lifestyle. While you can eat unhealthy food while doing intermittent fasting, eating healthy foods contribute towards living a long and healthy life. Therefore, be sure to include fruits, nuts, vegetables, healthy fats, and lean proteins in your diet.

Know when to quit. It is important that you're flexible and adapts to your changing needs. For instance, if your plan is to fast for 16 hours, but you begin feeling tired, you might as well shorten your day. You may also be working out, but you generally feel you don't have enough energy, this is also a reason to break your fast early. You shouldn't aim to be perfect at the expense of your wellbeing. If you begin feeling sick during your fasting window, it's also a good reason to cut short your fasting and pay attention to you your health. It's better to be consistent than to be perfect.

Keep it simple. Unlike many other diets that are designed to help in losing weight, intermittent fasting doesn't require you to deviate from your usual meals to some sophisticated menus. Therefore, aim at eating your usual meals during your eating window. However, you can also consider combining your intermittent fasting regimen with a low carb-high fat diet comprising real whole foods.

Get enough rest. Fasting, by itself, is not enough if you want to embrace a healthy lifestyle. Make sure you're also getting enough sleep. Your body requires sleep to be able to carry out some of the important functions. Therefore, don't work at night unless it's important. We aren't wired as other nocturnal beings; thus, we need to follow through our circadian rhythm. When you get sound sleep at night, no doubt your body will be able to fight off the weight in a better way even as your stress and cholesterol levels improve. If anything, intermittent fasting puts emphasis on giving the body adequate sleep. Make sure you plan your day so that you free up some time for good sleep. Most importantly, make sure you rest more when you fast for extended periods.

Practice perseverance. It's unfortunate that most people that have a problem with their weight are also impatient. This is probably because they're already under pressure to lose weight, yet it's just not happening. Moreover, most people trying to lose weight have already tried other ways of shedding off excess fat unsuccessfully and are looking for quick results. Unfortunately, intermittent fasting is not an overnight success. It takes time and consistency before you can see the results. You must be ready to see the change happen after a while since you're correcting problems/weight that has accumulated over the years. Don't lose hope in the process because by quitting, you can't tell whether you had made any progress. You can stall hunger by laughing, running, or talking to friends or engage in activities that stall hunger.

Hydrate during fasting. It's extremely important always to make sure you're drinking up enough during intermittent fasting. Yet it's common to find beginners thinking that they should not actually consume anything during the fasting window. This is wrong because intermittent fasting allows you to take water, tea, or coffee as long as you don't use any cream, milk, or sugar. Staying hydrated is important in extending your feeling of satiety; thus drinking water will help you to get rid of that feeling of hunger.

Manage your fasting time properly. It's a common thing for people to mismanage time during the fasting window just as is with our normal schedules. You need to know that not managing your fasting time well is likely to be a cause of distress. This can make your journey of losing weight painful and difficult. Stop thinking about food the entire time you're in the fasted state. This will create problems since your gut will be confused. You can manage your fasting time by staying busy while making sure that you're engaged until the last leg of your fasting window. When you're idle, it's likely that you'll only be thinking about food. Think about ways of putting off hunger. After all, our bodies have ample energy reserves that can run without food for a long time.

Don't rush the process. We all want quick results, but with intermittent fasting, you have to follow through the process. Don't attempt to make quick jumps because the body doesn't work this way. The transition process of your body is quite slow. Thus, you need to allow more time to adjust to change that comes with intermittent fasting. To succeed with each of these processes, make sure you stay at every stage for some time. This gives your body time to adjust to the changes. Remember, you're trying to change habits that are decades old, so you need to be patient to make your body adjust to the process. The other thing you must remember is that fasting is different in men and women. While a man's system is rugged and doesn't get to be affected by periods of extended fasting, fasting can affect a woman's health adversely; hence, it takes time to normalize. Hence, the need to start small and advance with time.

Have realistic expectations. It's okay to have a goal and dreams about your weight loss goals. Even then, make sure that you're grounded in reality. This is a good place to start as you're able to accept facts and avoid lots of disappointments. Having unrealistic expectations often contributes to the failure to recognize the benefits you derive from the process. For instance, if your goal is losing weight, then you must really think about the amount of time, you'll put into fasting and your overall commitment. Not taking all the relevant factors into consideration will leave you feeling frustrated and difficult to achieve the results you desire.

Determine how long you want to fast/create a routine. Since intermittent fasting is more of a pattern of eating than a diet fad, you can only get the best results when you follow it in routine. This means that you will not get the results if you're only practicing fasting in a way that is unstructured. If anything, doing intermittent fasting in an irregular manner will not yield any results; rather, it'll leave you feeling hungry. Your gut releases the hunger hormone with so much accuracy. As such, the gut is able to sense the time when you eat so that you feel gurgling in your stomach around exactly the same time the next day. This means that if you're keeping a 14-hour fast regularly, you'll notice you feel hungry hunger just about the time you need to break your fast. This means that if you don't keep a regular routine, then this will not happen. Making intermittent fasting a usual routine will help you get over the hassle of being too conscious. After a while, this would be part of your lifestyle hence easy to follow.

Don't be greedy when it's time to breaking your fast. Food is the most alluring thing you can come across when you've been deprived of it for long hours. It's actually tempting. You need to make sure that you don't get greedy when breaking your fast, rather get off the fast in a proper manner. The biggest mistake you can make is eating a lot as it can lead to various problems among them poor digestion. Your gut can be dry after long periods of fasting. Thus, stuffing it with heavy food can result in problems. When breaking your fast start with liquid food, slowly transitioning to semi-solid and finally solid foods. You also need to check the quantity of food that you eat because the brain takes time to decode the leptin signals that you're full. When the brain finally signals you're full, you'll have overeaten. This means that you need to eat slowly so that your brain has enough time to determine your satiety levels. Alternatively, stop eating when you're at 80% full after which you're unlikely to feel hungry again.

You only require a few calories during intermittent fasting because your body is running on just a few calories or no food at all for a longer period than usual. This can result in having a hangover initially. You can train your body to come with the stress that is linked to food deprivation in order to get used to staying for long without food. If you realize that you can't cope with your intermittent fasting plan, then you can consider switching to another plan. You might have chosen a plan that is not suitable for your needs or lifestyle. Don't be discouraged if one plan doesn't work. Rather, make sure you work towards finding the right fasting protocol that you'll be comfortable with while getting the results you need.

By transitioning into intermittent slowly, you're giving your body a chance to self-regulate and gradually adapt to your eating pattern that is changing. It also helps in diminishing or avoiding symptoms of early transition that include dry mouth, insomnia, and digestive changes.

Chapter 10: Common Myths About Intermittent Fasting

Before joining the intermittent fasting bandwagon, it is important to have a clear picture of what it is you're getting into and the kind of results you should expect. Like with any other programs, there are several misconceptions and myths associated with the intermittent fasting lifestyle that is as popular as the benefits. Let's debunk some of the myths about this eating pattern so that you feel more confident embarking on this weight loss and wellness strategy:

You'll definitely lose weight. While one of the primary reasons why most people take on intermittent fasting is to lose weight, the results are not guaranteed. Several factors come into play. Thus, intermittent fasting will not always lead to weight loss. This is especially true if you're fasting faithfully while at the same time throwing down pizza, candy, and burgers. Intermittent fasting works well when you're on a healthy diet. Don't treat your eating window like a cheat day and expect to see positive results.

Intermittent fasting will slow down your metabolism. There's a general fear that when you go into intermittent fasting, your metabolism slows down. This is not actually true because intermittent fasting doesn't restrict the number of calories you take. Rather, it makes you wait for a few hours before you can have your first meal. This doesn't make a difference in your metabolic rate. Instead, changes in your metabolic rate will only come about when you're not eating enough, which is not the case with intermittent fasting.

You can eat as much food during your feeding window. It's not exactly true that you can eat as much as you want during your feeding window. Here's the thing. When you start intermittent fasting, your aim should be entering a healthier lifestyle. Unfortunately, most people only go into it to lose weight before going back to their reckless eating at the end of the fast. Experts warn that this is counterproductive to the results you've attained during your fasting window. The key to success with intermittent fasting is eating normally when you end your fast so that you don't negate the time spent fasting.

It's better to fast than snack for weight loss. Most conventional diet regimens recommend snacking in between meals. Those who opt for intermittent fasting think it should be a substitute for snacking. Ultimately, weight loss is occasioned by a constant deficit in calories. Whether those calories are consumed within a four to eight-hour window or spread throughout the day is not an issue. Instead, you should aim to do what is beneficial to your body.

Intermittent fasting for weight loss is far much better compared to other weight loss strategies. If you believe that intermittent fasting is the best strategy for your weight loss, you need to think again. It is important to keep in mind that intermittent fasting is simply about exercising caloric restriction in terms of when you take your food. If anything, there's no evidence to prove that intermittent fasting works better than the other methods and means of losing weight. It all boils down to your approach and discipline.

You can't skip breakfast. You must have heard this one even with other diets that are designed to help in weight loss. It's largely believed that breakfast if is the most important meal of the day hence must be taken even during intermittent fasting. In fact, this is part of the American tradition. Although you'll be told you need to consume a good breakfast to get fuel for the day, this is not necessarily true. If anything, it's likely that you don't have an appetite when they wake up. However, you can always listen to your body and have a small breakfast. Depending on the intermittent fasting protocol you choose, you can always have your meals at a time of day when its convenient.

Skipping breakfast makes you fat. It's believed that when you skip breakfast, you'll experience excessive hunger and cravings that lead to weight gain. While a number of studies have linked skipping breakfast to obesity, this is not the case with intermittent fasting. However, another 2014 study conducted between obese adults who skipped breakfast and those who didn't find any difference in weight. That is, there's no difference in weight loss whether you eat breakfast or not. Eating breakfast can have benefits, but it's not essential.

You can't work out when you're fasting. Contrary to popular belief that you can't work out when you're fasting, you can carry on with your work out routine when fasting. In fact, working out when fasting is a positive thing. It is believed that working out on an empty stomach, especially when it is the first thing you do in the morning is more rewarding. This is because you'll be burning stored fat instead of using up the calories from the food you just consumed. You can then eat your breakfast after working out to replenish your body.

All fasting is the same, and everyone gets the same results. There are many forms of intermittent fasting that you can follow. There's no official fasting protocol leaving the flexibility of choosing what works for you. Therefore, you can opt to fast daily while someone else fasts for on alternate days. Consequently, you can be sure that everyone will get results that are unique to them depending on the fasting protocol they're following and their goal.

Fasting makes you extremely fit and healthy. Intermittent fasting in itself is not a magic bullet to achieving health and fitness. You'll do well to combine your eating pattern with proper care and exercise. You must work to maintain health and fitness in your entire life. They should not be taken for granted. Fasting alone will not give you an ideal body overnight. Moreover, when you lose excess weight, you'll have to make sure you continue maintaining it with healthy eating habits that include regular exercise and a nutritious diet.

Intermittent fasting is productive because the body doesn't process food at night. Although it's a common misconception that your body doesn't process food at night, it's actually the reason you lose weight during intermittent fasting. Your body is wired to digest food no matter the time. However, when you allow the body a certain time, usually between 12 and 18 hours, the focus shifts to other metabolic processes like cellular repair and autophagy taking the attention from digestion. Your body will digest food even if you eat at 3a.m.

Intermittent fasting will decrease your training performance. One of the fears most people have when contemplating intermittent fasting is a decrease in training performance. This because of the possibility of having to skip or having a light pre-workout meal. The truth is that a closer look at athletes who train while in the fasted state have not experienced any hindrance to their performance due to nutrient deprivation. Moreover, it's important to keep in mind that intermittent fasting doesn't deprive the body of fluids and water.

Intermittent fasting will lead to loss of muscle mass. The fact that you've reduced the frequency of eating especially proteins doesn't mean your body is in the catabolic state as it is largely assumed. The idea that fasting reduces muscle mass is based on the idea that your body relies on a constant supply of amino acids to maintain, build, or repair muscle tissue. It is important to keep in mind that when you have a large meal of protein at your last meal prior to your 16-20 hour fast, your body is likely to be releasing the amino acids they need by the time you break the fast. It's common to have a complete meal that digests proteins slowly to the time you have your next meal. The thing is that fasting for extended periods will cause muscle loss only when you are not eating a large balanced diet during your feeding window.

Eating big meals with a lot of carbohydrates in the evening causes weight gain. Most fitness and nutrition experts will link carbs to insulin. While this is correct, there's a tendency to overgeneralize the psychological effects of insulin. The fear is that an increase in insulin, especially in the evening, will result in the conversion of nutrients to fats because insulin sensitivity is highest in the morning and lowest at night.

Fasting leads to glorified, binge eating, and bulimia disorders. This is another ridiculous claim that has been continually advanced about intermittent fasting by classifying it as disordered eating. The truth is that with intermittent fasting, the time you eat is not as important as meeting your daily macronutrient and calorie goals. What this means is that you're able to stick to your diet. Moreover, fasting presents a number of health benefits that disqualify the idea of promoting binge eating and bulimia. Besides, it's unrealistic to expect someone who is on an intermittent fasting protocol not to eat a large meal. Eating a large meal does not necessarily equal to binge eating, especially if you're staying within your nutrient needs.

Intermittent fasting has limited uses in limited populations. This myth in itself suggests that intermittent fasting is less applicable to the majority. This is not true because most of the people that have found success with intermittent fasting will attest to the fact that it's such a huge relief from having to constantly obsess about following the clock all day just to make sure that you're eating after every 3 hours. Intermittent fasting is most likely to work well with most people's routines, especially if you're working. Not many people like to have a large meal in the morning or at midday owing to the nature of their schedules.

Eating frequently will help reduce hunger. Some people, especially those that are keen on following conventional weight loss diets, believe that when you snack in between meals, you'll prevent excessive hunger and cravings. Well, knowing when to eat is far much better because you get to eat one large meal that is packed with nutrients; hence, you'll experience satiety for longer periods. If anything, there's no evidence to show that snacking will reduce hunger.

Fasting puts your body in starvation mode. A common argument against intermittent fasting is that it can activate the starvation mode. That is, failure to eat will make your body assume it's starving hence shut down metabolism and the ability to burn fat. Long term weight loss reduces the calories you burn, which can aptly be described as starvation mode. Even then, this tends to happen whenever you're trying to lose weight regardless of the method you're using. There's no evidence that this is more with intermittent fasting. Evidence points to the fact that fasting for short term can increase metabolic rate.

Intermittent fasting is not for people with diabetes. Findings of a recent study point to the fact that intermittent fasting will result in improved weight loss, fasting blood sugar, and stabilize blood sugar after dinner in group 2 diabetics. In some instances, prolonged fasting will restore your insulin sensitivity, especially in type 2 diabetes. When your insulin sensitivity is improved, your body will produce less insulin and experience less inflammation. This shows intermittent fasting is important for individuals with diabetes by reducing the risk of kidney and heart disease.

There are many myths about intermittent fasting. While some have merit, others are outrightly wrong. For most people, intermittent fasting presents real benefits. It's one of the best tools to lose weight.

Chapter 11: Common mistakes people make While Intermittent Fasting

Although it is billed as the most effective method of losing weight, you can easily have difficulty with intermittent fasting. Research has found intermittent fasting to have a 31% drop out rate. There are many mistakes people make when making a switch from your regular eating plan to intermittent fasting. This can jeopardize your expectations by influencing the results because you might not see the results everyone is raving about, resulting in giving up. Having a workable and realistic approach to intermittent fasting can be the difference between your success and failure. Here are some of the common pitfalls you're likely to be making in your intermittent fasting:

Having a wrong plan for your lifestyle. Intermittent fasting is flexible; hence, you have the liberty of selecting a plan that suits your lifestyle. You need to understand the dynamics of the different forms of intermittent fasting to make sure you choose what will work well with your lifestyle, needs, and schedule. By signing up for a plan that you can't keep up with, you're definitely setting yourself up for failure. For instance, if you're working in a full-time job, have an intense workout routine and an active family, the 5:2 plan will not be realistic instead of the 16:8 plan will be more sensible and easier to maintain because you'll have a reasonable feeding window. Therefore, take time to do your research and pick a plan that will work well for you, and you're able to stick with comfortably.

Getting into intermittent fasting too soon. One of the reasons most people give up on diets is because it presents a departure from the natural and normal way of eating. As such, you'll find it impossible to keep up with. This is often the case when you jump into intermittent fasting too fast. For instance, if you're accustomed to eating after every 2-3 hours, it's unrealistic to switch to a 24-hour fast suddenly. As a beginner, you can begin by fasting for 12 hours and have a 12-hour eating window. This comes close to your regular pattern. You can then extend your fasting window gradually until you reach your goal. It takes time to stop feeling hungry when you take on intermittent fasting. This way, you'll find better success. The secret is to be patient and see a lifestyle change

Eating too much during the eating window. Although you don't have to count calories as is typical with most diets, intermittent fasting requires discipline in terms of determining how much you should eat. While it's true that you may be too hungry from too many hours of fasting, caution must be taken so that you don't overeat during your eating window. In fact, you try not to be preoccupied with your next meal because this can lead to binge eating. Instead, consider sitting down to a larger meal that is more satisfying so that you're not completely famished when you enter your feeding window. When you do this correctly, you won't feel too hungry during the fasting window to want to eat everything.

Failure to hydrate adequately. Although your intermitted fasting plan alternates patterns of eating and fasting, you must make sure that you're taking in enough water. You actually need to have a bottle of water by your side because you're missing out on the water from veggies and fruits. Failure to stay dehydrated can results in headaches and cramps while worsening hunger pangs. You can also have tea or coffee but without sugar. You don't want to take any sweetened drink that can have an effect on your insulin levels and stimulate your appetite giving you the desire to eat. Avoid fluids that are filled with proteins since they can halt autophagy that you need to promote during fasting. If you find drinking up difficult, you can consider using an app to ensure you're sipping up in between your fasting and feasting windows.

Overlooking what you're while focusing on when you're eating. While it's true that intermittent fasting is more of time centered eating regimen with no specific rules on what you should eat, your goal should be to eat healthy, nutrient dense foods. Therefore, you should not dwell on milkshakes, French fries, and the likes in your diet as these can easily undo the gains of fasting. Shift your focus from treating yourself after hours of fasting to getting nutrient-dense foods that are nourishing. Generally, your meals should have a protein, complex carbs, fiber, and good fats. These will keep you feeling satiated and carry you through the fasting window while helping you to build muscle, feel energetic, and maintain a healthy brain.

Eating too little. While it is wrong to overeat during your feeding window, you should also not eat too little. Fasting affects the hormones that control your appetite leaving you feeling less hungry. Consequently, when you get to eat, you'll only eat a small portion of food and feel full. Even then, you need to be careful so that you don't consume too little because failure to eat enough will leave you feeling extremely hungry the next day so that you can end up feeling lethargic and unable to perform any work. Failure to eat adequate food will cannibalize your muscle mass, resulting in slowed down metabolism. Lack of metabolic muscle mass will sabotage your ability to maintain fat. Eventually, you may end up feeling the need to skip fasting or even give up on intermittent fasting altogether.

Leading a sedentary lifestyle. You may likely want to skip your workout session because you're used to having a pre-workout snack. Exercising when fasting will definitely seem foreign. Although it is advisable that you check with your doctor before exercising while intermittent fasting, it's safe to carry on with your exercise routine, albeit with some alterations. This is because your body has lots of stored energy in the form of stored fat that is used up when there's no food. Aim to keep up with your routine or consider low impact exercises like walking. For instance, if you're fasting overnight, you can exercise in the morning after which you can eat a protein-rich meal for better muscle build.

Obsessing over intermittent fasting. When your fasting, you might be inclined to decline invitations to parties or even opt out for dinner with friends. When this is the case, your intermittent fasting goal may not be sustainable. You can fix this by shifting your fasting schedule either backward or forward by a couple of hours on the days when you have a date with friends so that you can still enjoy your social life without being guilty or the fear of being left out. Remember, intermittent fasting as a lifestyle is flexible; hence, it has to fit in your special occasions.

Conclusion

Thank you for making it through to the end of *Intermittent Fasting for Women*, let's hope it was informative and able to provide you with all of the tools you need to achieve your goals whatever they may be.

The next step is to take action that will usher you into a new level of wellness. If you still need help getting started, you are likely to get better results by evaluating your current schedule before you can select an appropriate intermittent fasting plan that is realistic, to begin with. Remember, you'll not be doing this to please anyone but for your own benefit.

Intermittent fasting is a great concept of scheduling your meal times, not just for weight loss but also living holistically because it gives you access to numerous health benefits. What's more? Unlike many weight loss diets that are restrictive, expensive, and offer minimal results, intermittent fasting is free and easy to follow through. You simply need to change your eating pattern so that you have periods of fasting followed by periods of feasting.

This book is especially a great resource that will help you through your journey in carving a new lifestyle. Remember, you don't have to change your way of living but instead embrace the new way of feeding to suit your way of living. In fact, you can still carry on with your exercise routine even though you may have to tailor it to your current situation in terms of when you eat and how intense your workout is.

What are you waiting for? Go ahead and start preparing for your intermittent fasting experience to tap into its benefits. Use the information you have acquired in this book as a springboard to prepare and transform your life.

Intermittent Fasting 16/8 Mastery

The Bullet-Proof Program that Helped 3.479 Busy American People Gain a New Self

By

Austin Harris

Table of Contents

Part One

Introduction

While fasting is becoming more popular in the Western world at this time, the truth is that it has been an important aspect of human history, religion, protest, and health for thousands upon thousands of years. No matter where you look in the world, you are likely to find a history of fasting in nearly every culture. However, with the rise of modern foods, grocery stores, and convenience fewer people have taken to fasting. While it is certainly good that more people have access to food, it is a loss that most cultures have lost their practice of fasting.

It is never healthy to deprive your body of food. However, with fasting, you are able to schedule your meals in a way that your body is being fueled with all the needed nutrients while still making use of this powerful tool. Studies and thousands of years of experience have proven the beneficial effects of intermittent fasting. When you fast while still fueling your body between fasting periods you can boost your health, increase your longevity, prevent disease, and increase weight loss.

Intermittent fasting may be a new thought process for many individuals in the modern world, but there are many tools and resources that will make this journey easy and successful. Within the pages of this book, you will learn the many benefits of fasting, how to practice it successfully, the ways in which you can benefit your health, tips, and tricks to get the most out of fasting, and even recipes to eat between your fasting periods.

There is no reason to hesitate. With the tools within this book, you can succeed like never before. You can enjoy healthy and delicious meals while also losing weight and gaining health.

Chapter 1: The Impact of Obesity

Whether a person is curvy, chubby, fat, or any other term that they prefer, there is nothing to feel inferior about. Today's society focuses so much on weight rather than health that it leads to eating disorders and fat phobia. However, while there is nothing wrong with being curvy, it is important to address extreme fat gain, such as obesity. This is because when you gain so much weight to be medically diagnosed as obese you are at risk for many diseases, experience decreased energy, and suffer from a shortened lifespan. Thankfully, there is a way in which you can increase your health while losing fat in a healthy way. With intermittent fasting, you can focus on your health rather than your weight, and the fat will come off in the process.

Within this chapter, you will learn the effects of obesity, how it is different from being curvy or "fat", and the importance of managing healthy body weight.

Obesity is not about the way you look, fitting into society's limited expectations, or wearing a certain size of jeans. Instead, fighting obesity is about your overall health and avoiding disease and a limited lifespan. While many people believe that obesity is only caused by what you eat and how much you eat, this is far from the truth. Yes, your eating habits will affect your weight. However, your genetics, medication usage, physical activity, and much more can affect whether or not you are obese. After all, one person may eat junk food all the time and still be underweight; meanwhile, another person may eat only small amounts of healthy foods and still be medically obese. Thankfully, no matter your risk factors, whether it is your diet or genetics, intermittent fasting has been proven as effective in treating obesity.

Sadly, while obesity numbers used to be quite low, they have been steadily on the rise over the past few decades. It has now reached the point where over thirty-three percent of people are medically considered "seriously overweight". Sadly, fifteen percent of adolescents are also medically overweight. These numbers have been on the rise for so long, that America and other Western countries are in a dire state. Doctors and other health officials have concluded that while genetics and other factors play into weight gain, a large cause for this spike in weight gain is poor diet, decrease in exercise, and tobacco usage.

It is difficult for doctors to know when a person is at a healthy weight. This is because everyone's natural healthy physique is different. One person's ideal weight may be considered underweight at one-hundred pounds whereas another person's ideal weight may be considered overweight at one-hundred and eighty pounds. Every person's body is different because every person's DNA and cellular makeup is different. For this reason, doctors will use a measurement system that has standard weight categories, but they do this carefully. When a doctor measures a person's body, mass index (BMI) they know that while the scale may categorize them as "underweight" or "overweight" these categories are not steadfast and unbreakable classifications. This is because a person's BMI does not account for DNA, bone density, family history, diet, activity level, or anything else. The only data that BMI calculates a person's weight with is body weight compared to height. This means that while you can compare your body weight and height against the ideal "average", you are unable to use the BMI scale as an absolute standard. This scale is only one aspect out of multiple that a doctor uses to diagnose a person as either underweight, overweight, or obese.

If you want to learn your BMI number on the scale, you can either look at calculators online or ask your doctor. Keeping in mind that BMI does not along indicate health but must be used keeping other factors in mind; let's look at the BMI number scale:

- **Overweight**

- If a person is between 25-29.9 they are considered "overweight" on the BMI scale. At this weight, the excess fat is likely putting extra strain on their body, predisposing them to a number of diseases and health problems as they age.

- **Obesity**

- When a person reaches obesity range it is considered a disease that significantly lowers quality of life, increases illness, and decreases life expectancy. The BMI scale considered obesity to be between the range of 30-39.9.

- **Severe Obesity**

- When a person has a number of over 40 they are considered severely obese. At this weight, a person is over one-hundred pounds over a healthy weight. While it is possible to be healthy at other BMI levels, it is not possible at severe obesity. However, a person who is obese or severely obese should never be shamed. If you are one of these people, remember that you have value, you are worth the effort it takes to gain health, and nobody has the right to mock you. While you may be struggling with your weight, you worthwhile person and nobody (including yourself) should judge you. All you have to do is choose now to improve your health and life with intermittent fasting.

Now that you understand the basics of what obesity is and is not, let's have a look at some of the health effects of this condition. Remember, while it is true nobody should shame you for your weight and you can love your body no matter what, it is also true that obesity and severe obesity will greatly increase your risk of disease and early death. In fact, every year in America obesity causes approximately three-hundred-thousand premature deaths.

Type II Diabetes

The rates of diabetes, especially type II, have been on the rise for the last few decades. The numbers have risen to such a dangerous degree that between 1990 and 2015 the number of people in America with the disease more than tripled. Sadly, as of 2017, the American Centers For Disease Control found that over one-hundred-million Americans are suffering from diabetes or pre-diabetes. Type II diabetes is most often caused by obesity, as obesity triggers the body to become resistant to insulin and increases blood sugar, both of which are the main factor of diabetes. Even if a person is only slightly obese, it greatly increases this risk of developing type II diabetes.

High Blood Pressure and Heart Disease

When the body is carrying excess fat the body must increase its blood circulation, in order to provide the increase in cells oxygen to live. Without this increase of blood circulation and oxygen consumption, your body's tissue would begin to rot. Therefore, to prevent the decaying of cells the heart is forced into increasing its workload, putting stress on your heart and added pressure to the walls of your arteries. This results in high blood pressure, which gradually causes damage to your heart and arteries while decreasing your body's ability to transport blood to the cells effectively. This increase in workload due to excess fat is why three out of four causes of high blood pressure are a result of obesity. Not only does this high blood pressure cause damage on its own, but it also predisposes a person to kidney disease, coronary heart disease, stroke, and congestive heart failure.

Respiratory Disorders

As you have learned when you are obese, your heart is forced to overwork in order to provide these excess cells with oxygen. However, there is another problem with this, which is that when a person is obese they have a reduced lung capacity. This means that it is more difficult to get enough oxygen, and can even cause other lung disorders. People with obesity are four times more likely to develop asthma than those without obesity, and other respiratory disorders and infections are common, as well.

Over half of the population with obesity also develops obstructive sleep apnea. This is a dangerous condition, which causes a person to stop breathing during their sleep. Obstructive sleep apnea is caused due to excess fat in the airways, throat, tongue, and neck causing a blockage while a person is asleep. A person with sleep apnea can stop breathing hundreds of times a night, and not even realize that this is occurring. Even though a person may be unaware that they have sleep apnea, it leads to many complications such as fatigue, reduced blood oxygen, high blood pressure, abnormal heart heartbeats, recurrent heart attacks, stroke, and even vehicle accidents.

Joint and Bone Damage

Whether it is osteoarthritis, gout, chronic back pain, spine disorders, or disc herniation, obesity is known to cause damage to both the joints and bones. Often times, when a person has added weight they develop osteoarthritis in their knees and hips causing prolonged stress. This not only causes chronic pain but often leads to joint replacement surgery as a person ages.

Cancer

While anyone may develop cancer, studies have shown that your weight can greatly increase or reduce your risk of developing this devastating disease. In fact, doctors believe that obesity may cause up to ninety-thousand cancer deaths in America yearly. The higher your BMI level is the more at risk you are of developing and dying of cancer. This includes many types of cancer, such as thyroid, kidney, liver, prostate, ovarian, pancreatic, breast, leukemia, and more. Obese women with cancer are fifty-two times more likely to die of cancer than a woman at a healthy weight, and men are shockingly sixty-two times more likely. This is why if you develop cancer it is important to focus on your diet and weight. Not only that, if you hope to avoid cancer (especially if you have a family history) it is vital that you focus on maintaining healthy body weight.

Not only does obesity affect your health, but it will also impact your wallet. This is because obesity causes a person to undergo more medical care, which cost Americans one-hundred and forty-seven billion dollars in 2008. If you want to protect your health, increase your quality of life, prevent premature death, and save money you can do all of this and more by creating a healthier body weight with intermittent fasting.

Chapter 2: What Intermittent Fasting Entails

Intermittent fasting is much different than skipping meals when you are busy. This is because intermittent fasting is done systematically, ensuring you still eat enough and the nutrients your body requires. With this approach you also control when you do and don't eat, allowing you to ensure you never go too long without meals. In this chapter, we will go over the fundamentals of intermittent fasting, so that you can fully understand what it entails.

First, it is important to understand that fasting is not a new practice. There is much historical evidence of people using it for not only their health but also for their religion or political causes. For instance, the ancient Greeks' would use fasting to improve poor health.

For religious reasons, Buddhist monks frequently avoid eating after twelve in the afternoon, which is a form of intermittent fasting. They will also practice fasting during periods of meditation and study.

In the Hindu religion, there are many types of fasting as well as various customs. The exact way a person fasts will vary, as there are different beliefs and customs based on a person's individual beliefs and the local customs of where they live. For some individuals, this means that they limit how much food they eat during the day. Others may avoid eating or drinking anything from an hour before sunset, until an hour after sunrise. Often times, these fasts correlate with religious festivals and holidays, such as Purnima, Ekadashi, and Pradosha.

Many Muslims who are able to participate in Ramadan, a sacred month which is meant to purify both body and soul. Not only does this increase their consciousness of God, but it also is meant to improve their health by decreasing excess food intake and overindulgence. By fasting in this way, the participants are also able to control their impulses, allowing them to eat fewer unhealthy foods and prevent over-consumption.

While not all Christians practice fasting, there are certain denominations within Western Christianity that do practice this method. Those within the Catholic, Anglican, Methodist, or Reformed denominations are all more likely to make use of fasting and its benefits. The most common time of fasting is during Lent, which is a forty-day period in which individuals focus on Christ and His time of trials in the desert.

Religious Jews also participate in fasts, as there are six days of fasting throughout the year. The most notable example is Yom Kippur, in which every male above the age of thirteen and every female above the age of twelve is expected to fast. During this fasting period, not only do they avoid food, but they also avoid all drinks, including water.

For political reasons, people have frequently utilized hunger strikes for thousands of years. Fasting in the way of hunger strikes has been used for thousands of years. Archaeologists have even found evidence of people practicing hunger strikes in India in order to protest during seven-hundred BC. Hunger strikes have also been utilized in Ireland, England, America, and many other countries across the world.

Now that you understand the historical basis of intermittent fasting, let's look at the basics of the fasted state, some of the more common types of fasting, and correct a couple of common misconceptions.

The fasted state is a powerful ability your body takes on when you have not eaten. The difference between the fasted and fed state is what makes intermittent fasting so effective. Sadly, despite these scientifically proven results, many people are unaware of the powerful abilities afforded to them. This is largely due to misconceptions and old wives tales that have been passed through the generations, despite being disproved. Thankfully, if a person is willing to learn and overcome their preconceived misconceptions they can learn the powerful effects that are possible with fasting and how to best make use of them.

After you have eaten a meal, even if it was only a single bite of cake, you enter what is known as the fed state. This state lasts various lengths of time, depending on what was eaten, a person's metabolism, and more. However, generally, this stage lasts between three to five hours. During this time frame, your body is working to digest food, absorb nutrients, and deliver these nutrients to all the cells that require them. During this time, you are unable to burn your body's fat tissues, as your body is instead attempting to process the food you have eaten. Your insulin will also be higher during this time, which is another aspect that prevents weight loss. It is easy to see that if you eat frequent meals so that you are often in a fed state, you will be unable to lose weight.

Between the fed state and the fasted state, you have another ability that merges the two states together. This is the post-absorptive state, which occurs after the three to five-hour mark of the fed state. During this time your insulin levels lower and you are no longer in the process of digesting or absorbing nutrients. When you are in this state you are able to lose weight, unlike in the fed state.

Approximately twelve hours after eating you enter the final phase, which is the fasted state. While throughout history people would naturally enter the fasted state when they were hard at work, in modern society, this is uncommon unless we are practicing fasting for religious reasons. It is a good thing that in today's society people get breaks at work; however, if we always avoid fasting then we will also be avoiding its many benefits. For instance, people who practice intermittent fasting are often able to lose weight even if they don't change any other lifestyle factors. Even if a person continues to eat the same, doesn't increase or begin to exercise, and sleeps the same, they are still able to burn off their stored fat tissues and lose weight. This is because when you enter the fasted state your body will naturally have to burn off the fat within your tissues for energy since you are not providing it with food at the moment.

Yet, just because you are not feeding your body constantly does not mean you are depriving it. After all, since you are in control of intermittent fasting you are able to feed your body all of its needed calories and nutrients on a strategic schedule. Fasting is not an unnatural or unhealthy process. Instead, it is an incredible ability that powers our bodies when used correctly. There is a common misconception that fasting is the same is starving your body, which is not true. When your body is starved it is completely deprived of the nutrients and calories it requires. However, with fasting, you ensure your body gets everything it needs so that it is always operating at its best.

For instance, if you eat a large healthy dinner at 6 pm there is nothing wrong with waiting until 6 am or even 12 pm before you eat your next meal. In fact, breakfast was originally known as "breaking fast", as it is when you break your nighttime fast from when you were asleep. This is a normal everyday process for most people, and it can be used to benefit your health and weight. Remember, life requires balance, which means you shouldn't constantly be fasting or eating. You can balance the two so that you can be in a fed state for approximately half of your day, and fasting the remaining half.

Please keep in mind that if you have an eating disorder that intermittent fasting is not a good idea. While it is a perfectly healthy lifestyle, a person with an eating disorder does not need to worry about food schedules. A good example of why this is not good is that you wouldn't offer an alcoholic glass of wine, even a single glass with dinner. While you may be offering the alcoholic a single glass of wine, we all know that alcoholics are unable to drink a single glass, and will end up back in the midst of addiction. The same is true for people with eating disorders. While intermittent fasting is healthy and natural, for a person with an eating disorder it can promote thoughts of returning to their addicting behaviors. Therefore, only people without eating disorders should pursue intermittent fasting.

Now that you have an understanding of the fasted and fed states, let's have a quick look at the most common forms of intermittent fasting. These will just be short synopses so that you can get a better picture of fasting. We will cover these methods (and more) in further detail later on.

12/12 Method

The shortest fast is the twelve-hour method. With this fasting, a person spends half of their day in the fed state, known as an eating window, and a half in the fasted state. This is the perfect fast for beginners, as it is relatively small, and many people may already naturally fast for this length of time between dinner and breakfast. However, because this fast is shorter it does not allow you as much time in the fasting state. Remember, the fasted state only begins after approximately twelve hours, meaning that as soon as you enter the fasted state you are once again eating.

With this method, you will not experience as many benefits, but it is a good way to dip your toes into the pool of fasting during the beginning.

Meal Skipping Method

Another great method for beginners is meal skipping. With this method of fasting, you eat a generally healthy diet and simply skip a meal a few times a week when you find yourself not hungry. For instance, if you wake up one morning and find yourself satisfied, then you can go ahead and skip breakfast and wait for lunch.

16/8 Method

The method we will explore the most during this book in later chapters is the 16/8 fast. With this method, you enjoy an eight-hour eating window with a sixteen-hour fasting phase. This method is effective as it is not overly long, but it allows your body enough time in the fasted state to burn fat and increase your health.

5:2 Method

With the five-two method a person will eat normally for five days a week, but two separate days a week they will fast. For instance, they may eat normally for most of the week, but then on Tuesdays and Thursdays, they choose to fast. On fasting days, a woman will consume no more than five-hundred calories and a man no more than six-hundred calories. These calories mean that a person won't be in the fasted state for the full twenty-four hours, but they will help the person to feel satisfied and energized.

24-Hour Method

Similar to the 5:2 method is the twenty-four-hour fast. However, with this fasting method, a person does not consume any calories during the fast, not even a small snack. Because of this, the twenty-four-hour fast is more extreme but also helps a person with more weight loss and health benefits. To make this fast easier, a person should start it midway through a day instead of at the beginning of the day. For instance, a person may fast from 2 pm on Wednesday to 2 pm on Thursday. With this, a person's fast will be a full twenty-four hours, but they will still be able to eat breakfast and lunch prior to beginning their fast.

Chapter 3: The Health Benefits

There is much scientific interest in the health benefits of intermittent fasting. One such example is the Johns Hopkins School of Medicine, which has explored the options fasting provides. For instance, the Professor of Neuroscience at Johns Hopkins, Mark Mattson, who is also chief of the Laboratory of Neurosciences at the National Institute of Aging, has examined the effects of fasting on neurodegenerative diseases. During his research, Dr. Mattson found that not only do excess calories affect your body's weight, but they also affect your brain health. In fact, you can be at a healthy weight and your brain will still be negatively affected by the consumption of excess calories, even if your waistline isn't.

During the course of his research, Dr. Mattson found that by cutting food consumption several days a week we greatly decrease our risk of developing damaging diseases to our brains, such as Alzheimer's and Parkinson's disease. Not only will it decrease our risk of developing these diseases in the future, but it can also improve our memory and mood in the present.

In his time of the study, Dr. Mattson analyzed decades worth of research on the ties between brain function, caloric intake, and fasting. This enabled him to discover that by practicing fasting at least two days a week a person can greatly improve their neural connections within the hippocampus. It was also found that it could protect the brain's neurons from plaque that causes Alzheimer's disease.

Along with finding these benefits, Dr. Mattson also discovered that fasting cannot be replaced with calorie restriction. The body undergoes specific conditions while in a fasted state, such as ketone body production, that does not occur when a person is simply restricting calories. Therefore, if you want to improve your health there is no replacement to multi-weekly intermittent fasting.

As you have learned, being overweight and obese takes a great toll on your health. Therefore, if you want to improve your health it is important to get to healthy body weight. For people who are overweight, this means that it's vital to losing weight, every single pound makes a difference. While calorie restriction often leaves people fatigued, hungry, and at their wit's end, the same is not true of intermittent fasting. This method is also more effective than calorie restriction, as your body is better able to burn fat when in a fasted state, boosting your metabolism and increasing weight loss-promoting hormones.

In one study, it was sound that by practicing a twenty-four-hour fast a person can lose up to nine percent of their body weight. When these people continued to participate in intermittent fasting over a period of months their weight loss continued, as well. This is beneficial, as calorie restriction alone often causes a person to develop stalls in weight loss, which is less common with intermittent fasting.

Another study found that intermittent fasting without calorie restrictions was equally as effective as continuous calorie restriction when practiced for a period of weeks. During this study, participants lost up to eight percent of their body weight and sixteen percent of their body fat. This is all while the fasting group enjoyed whatever foods they wanted without restrictions during their non-fasting hours.

The human growth hormone (HGH) is a vital aspect of weight loss, metabolism, and muscle strength. In short, if we want to improve these three aspects of our health we should focus on increasing this hormone. Luckily, fasting has been shown to trigger an increase in HGH, greatly boosting your overall weight loss and muscle health.

In one study on HGH and fasting, it was found that eleven healthy people greatly increased their levels of human growth hormone when they fasted for a twenty-four-hour period. In another study, it was found that when men fasted for forty-eight hours their HGH increased to a significant degree.

Studies have found that insulin affects HGH levels. Since fasting maintains healthy insulin and blood sugar levels for prolonged periods of time, this can optimize HGH levels so that they can best be used.

Speaking of insulin, the ability of fasting to manage insulin and blood sugar is especially helpful for people with type II diabetes or pre-diabetes. This can help many people, such as those in a study on the matter. During the course of the study, the participants with type II diabetes found that their blood sugar levels had reduced significantly when practicing intermittent fasting for short time periods, greatly improving their condition.

Another study found that regular intermittent fasting is as effective as calorie restriction when it comes to reducing insulin resistance. This is great news, as insulin resistance causes weight gain, type II diabetes, and more.

Inflammation is an important part of the immune system, which helps to heal injuries and prevents the infection of germs when we get a wound. However, levels of high inflammation that continue without cause are known as chronic inflammation. While inflammation may be necessary and helpful at times, in excess it becomes harmful, increasing joint pain as well as diseases such as rheumatoid arthritis, heart disease, and even cancer.

However, much to the relief of those suffering from abnormally or chronically high inflammation levels, intermittent fasting has been shown to manage inflammation levels to something much more healthy. This allows your body to use inflammation, as it should while you are injured and preventing an excess of inflammation when it is unneeded.

In one such study, fifty adults practiced regular intermittent fasting for an entire month. It was shown that those who participated experienced a significant decrease in inflammation, as was proven by their inflammatory blood markers. Another study found the same results when participants practiced daily twelve-hour fasts for a month.

One of the leading causes of death worldwide is heart disease, accounting for approximately thirty-one percent of deaths across the globe. It may feel like there is little to nothing we can do about heart disease, especially if we have a long family history of this devastating condition. Thankfully, we can take our heart health into our own hands. Studies have found that by changing our lifestyle we can greatly impact our heart health for the better. One way in which we can do this is by practicing regular intermittent fasting.

In one such study, it was found that by practicing alternate-day fasting for a total of two months individuals were able to greatly reduce their harmful LDL cholesterol by twenty-five percent and blood triglycerides by thirty-two percent. This change is significant, as by dropping LDL cholesterol and blood triglycerides by a quarter and a third respectfully a person is able to greatly reduce their risk of a heart-related event as they age. Whether you are predisposed to heart disease or not, you will benefit from this improvement.

In another study, ten individuals were able to not only decrease their LDL cholesterol and blood triglycerides but also their total cholesterol levels and blood pressure. Lastly, one study analyzed over four-thousand and six-hundred individuals. In this study, it was found that those who regularly practice fasting have a lower risk of developing heart disease, coronary heart disease, and type II diabetes.

While the research on cancer-related benefits from intermittent fasting is limited, the research that is available is promising. For instance, one study found that when rats practice alternate-day fasting it prevents the growth and formation of cancerous tumors.

In another study, it was found that when cancer cells within test tubes are forced into several cycles of fasting that it is as equally effective in delaying tumor growth as chemotherapy. This study also found that fasting the cells increased how effective chemotherapy is on treating formed cancer cells. There may be multiple reasons for this effect, but one may be that cancer cells require glucose to grow. Usually, your body provides all cells (cancerous and non-cancerous) with glucose throughout the day as you partake in food and drinks. However, when you are fasting your body relies on fat, protein, and ketones for fuel instead of glucose. While your body's cells can make this change, cancer cells are unable to survive without glucose, therefore the cells are starved and unable to grow. Of course, while this is one reason for the beneficial effects of fasting when you have or want to prevent cancer, there may be other reasons that have yet to be researched.

At this point in time, the research on intermittent fasting's effects on cancer is limited. However, hopefully in the near future doctors and scientists will continue to research this promising field.

Epilepsy is when the brain develops a disorder, which causes frequent electrical misfirings. This escaped electricity can cause convulsions, damage to neurons, and much more. There are many types of epilepsy, and each type presents itself with its own symptoms. While one person may only present seizures a few times a year or a month, other people may be troubled with multiple seizures a day. This condition makes it unsafe to drive or enjoy many other common activities. In children, this can even cause a delay in normal development.

However, fasting has long been a proven treatment method for epilepsy. In fact, people have been treating epilepsy with long-term fasting for over a hundred years now. For many people, fasting may be able to take the place of medication. However, for others, it may help in conjunction when medication alone is insufficient.

While the research is limited, studies on animals have suggested that regularly practicing intermittent fasting may slow down aging and increase longevity. In one such study on rats, it was found that rats who practiced alternate-day fasting lived a shocking eighty-three percent longer than rats who do not fast. Other animal studies on the matter have been conducted, finding similar results.

As you can see, there are many benefits of regularly practicing fasting. Whether you hope to prevent neurodegenerative diseases, lower your cholesterol, treat insulin resistance, decrease chronic inflammation, slow down aging, or improve your longevity, you can benefit from intermittent fasting. It doesn't matter if you hope to overhaul your entire health system to improve your present or make a change now to improve your future; science has shown that you can achieve your goals with regular fasting.

Chapter 4: The Scientific Basis of Fasting

Intermittent fasting may seem like a simple process, after all, you are only going longer periods between meals. You can still eat the same number of calories and foods if you wish, though you will have even more success if you choose to also eat healthy meals. However, while intermittent fasting may appear simple on the outside, there is a chain reaction going on inside your body when in the fasted state. In this chapter, we will learn about this reaction in your body and how fasting affects your cells, hormones, and more.

Whenever you eat, even a single bite of food, your body reacts by releasing insulin. The purpose of this insulin is to convert any natural sugars (such as fructose and glucose) into fuel for the cells. If you have more fuel than your cells need, then insulin will also help to store the excess fuel as body fat. If you go extended periods of time without insulin spikes, such as when you are fasting, your body will realize it needs more fuel. Where does it get that fuel? From the body fat that the insulin has previously stored.

However, if a person develops insulin resistance their insulin levels will be constantly high, blood sugar will rise, and they will gain weight. This is the process of type II diabetes. When this happens, a person is unable to easily lose weight, as they constantly have spiked insulin, meaning their body never resorts to body fat for fuel. Thankfully, as you learned in the previous chapter, intermittent fasting can be used to treat both type II diabetes and insulin resistance. It can do this by giving the body a break from constant blood sugar and insulin spikes, allowing them to return to normal over time. As intermittent fasting helps to manage your insulin and blood sugar, it will naturally cause your body to resort to using its stored fat, allowing you to lose that stubborn weight.

The body has three types of food it converts into energy, which is protein, fat, and carbohydrates. These are converted into a variety of fuels. For instance, protein is converted into amino acids, fats into fatty acids, and carbohydrate into glucose. However, there are a couple of exceptions. During the process of fasting, a person will convert fatty acids into ketones and if a person burns off all the glucose in their body they will convert amino acids into glucose to fuel the brain cells.

Typically, the human body is most abundant with glucose as the main fuel source, with fatty and amino acids on the side. Yet, when a person is in a fasted state and no longer has glucose within their system the body will convert to a fat-dominated fuel source. This fuel source primarily burns off body fat. Not only that, but it will also produce ketones to fuel the few cells that are unable to utilize fat, and it will convert amino acids into glucose for the fewer still cells that are unable to use either fat or ketones. The exact amount of time it takes a person to enter this state varies from person to person, depending on how much glucose was in their system when they began their fast and whether or not they have insulin resistance.

Let's have a look at the body throughout the fed, post-absorptive, and fasted states:

1. **Fed State**

2. The fed state starts when you take a bite of any food. During this time, your insulin levels will rise in order to deliver glucose to your cells for energy. Any excess glucose is taken to the liver to be stored as glycogen, and any more than the liver can store is converted to fatty acids to be stored as body fat.

3. **Post-Absorptive Phase**

4. This stage of the cycle will vary greatly in terms of length. For most people, this phase lasts six to eight hours. However, it can last longer if a person ate an excess of food or if they have insulin resistance. During the post-absorptive phase, your body will begin to use the glucose within your cells and liver for energy.

5. **Gluconeogenesis Phase**

6. After your body has burned through all the glucose within your cells and liver it will begin to produce its own glucose if more is not provided for it. During this process your liver will take the amino acids from your body and transmute them into glucose, thereby allowing your brain to fuel the cells that

require glucose. These cells include some neurons, kidney medulla, and testicles. For non-diabetic people, blood sugar will drop while still remaining in a healthy range.

7. **Ketosis Phase**

8. Most people do not enter the ketosis phase during intermittent fasting, or at the very least not someone who has just begun the practice of fasting or someone who eats a lot of calorie-dense meals. This is because the ketosis process does not typically start until one to two days into a fast, and intermittent fasting never includes fasts that last longer than twenty-four-hours.

9. Although, if a person were to combine a low-carbohydrate and high-fat diet with intermittent fasting, then they would be in a continuous state of ketosis. During this process, the human body is best optimized to breakdown body fat for energy, as there has been a continuous flow of insulin for some time. This body fat, or triglycerides, are broken down into glycerol and fatty acids. The fatty acids are directly used as energy for most of the body's cells, whereas the glycerol can be transmuted into glucose through gluconeogenesis.

10. In order to reduce the number of amino acids and glycerol that need to be converted, the body will use fatty acids to produce ketones. Unlike fat, these ketones can cross the blood-brain barrier and therefore lessen the amount of glucose needed. Overall, ketones can lessen the amount of glucose required by seventy-percent.

11. **Protein Conservation Phase**

12. After a few days of fasting the protein conservation phase begins, in which the human growth hormone is elevated in order to maintain muscle mass. The main energy fuels to keep your body maintained is provided by ketones and fatty acids. In order to reduce the metabolic rate, the hormone adrenaline will increase.

Along with insulin, your body will also affect other aspects of your body's hormonal and cellular system. This is especially true of your hormones, in which the human growth hormone, adrenaline, and insulin are affected. These play an important role in a healthy body and weight loss. You already know how insulin is affected, so let's have a look at the two remaining hormones that we mentioned.

The human growth hormone is vital for weight loss, this is because it makes fats available and allows the body to better utilize them as a fuel source. Along with aiding with weight loss, it also protects our bone density and muscle mass, allowing us to maintain a healthy body as we lose weight. As a person ages, their production of the human growth hormone decreases, which is largely why the older a person gets the more they struggle to lose weight. However, with fasting, we can greatly increase the production of this important hormone, even if we are older. Studies have found that HGH can increase to five times its normal production during periods of fasting.

This increase in HGH allows a person to maintain their lean muscle mass while losing weight, better than is possible with calorie restriction. This is because it is the responsibility of HGH to maintain muscle mass, and this hormone is not increased during caloric restriction.

Adrenaline, otherwise known as noradrenaline, is a neurotransmitter hormone found in both the body and brain. When fasting, this hormone is increased to boost our energy. The purpose of this is to sustain us with energy between meals and so that if we are low on food we will still have the energy to go and get more to feed ourselves. This speeds up our metabolism, allowing us to continue going about our day despite the reduction in food. Many people worry that fasting will cause their metabolism to "shut down", but the opposite is, in fact, true, which is a great benefit to energy levels and weight loss!

It is noradrenaline that allows us to stretch out our meals, utilizing our body fat. Without this hormone, our system would constantly be putting away excess glucose as body fat without ever being able to rely on it. With this hormone we can make use of the fuel we put aside for a rainy day.

Chapter 5: Metabolic Autophagy, The Golden Key

While most people have never heard of autophagy (pronounced Aw-TOFF-uh-gee), it is an important metabolic function present in humans. The name originates from the Greek words "auto-" and "phagein", basically translating "eat thyself".

Don't worry, this does not mean that a person is literally eating themselves, but that our cells can consume other cells. The reason that it is largely unknown by today's adults is that it is a term that only has recent roots due to going long undiscovered. In this chapter, we will explore the discovery of autophagy, why it's the Golden Key of intermittent fasting, and the benefits it presents.

Back in the 1950's scientists started developing an understanding of autophagy, thanks to Christian de Duve, a Belgian scientist. A special compartment in human cells was discovered, known as an organelle, and this organelle was named "lysosome". In this organelle, there were enzymes whose purpose it is to help digest protein, fats, and carbohydrates. This special organelle was discovered by Dr. Duve, who was even given the Nobel Prize for his discovery.

As more research was conducted on lysosome over the following decade, it was found that this organelle was able to contain many other cells and organelles. Surprised by this find, the researchers were able to discover that there was a type of vehicle delivering other cells and organelles to the lysosome, which is then consumed. The new vehicle type that carries these cells were named "autophagosomes", and the process of the lysosome using the autophagosomes was termed "autophagy". It was Dr. Christian de Duve who coined these two new terms.

Forward a few years and throughout the 1970s and 1980s, researches sought to better understand another aspect of autophagy, although at the time they did not yet understand that the two were connected. This research discovered proteasome, which is another system that is used to breakdown old and unneeded proteins. However, while the researchers knew that this process could efficiently breakdown smaller proteins one-by-one, they didn't know what happened to larger and more complex proteins or old and over-used organelles.

Then, in the 1990s a researcher, Yoshinori Ohsumi, was focused on studying the effects of protein breakdown in the organelle "vacuole". This type of organelle closely relates to the lysosome. For his test, Mr. Ohsumi studied yeast cells. This is common, are similar to human cells, and can, therefore, help gene identification. However, the cells and inner structures of yeast are also smaller than human cells, making it more difficult to study under a microscope. Yet, Mr. Ohsumi didn't give up. Instead, he theorized that he could know whether or not the vacuole underwent autophagy by altering the yeast itself. By culturing a mutated version of yeast that contained protein sources that would not breakdown, Mr. Ohsumi was able to wait and witness a large number of autophagosomes gather within the cells. By preventing the protein breakdown it allowed for such a large number of autophagosomes to gather that it was discernible under the microscope. This result allowed Mr. Ohsumi to prove that autophagy is present within the cells of yeast, and more importantly, it allowed him to identify and characterized the genes responsible for the process.

Mr. Ohsumi published his initial results and then conducted a series of further studies on the subject. During these studies, he was able to continue to identify which genes are essential for the autophagy process and characterize the proteins encoded within the genes. He was even able to find that autophagy is controlled by various proteins, each of which regulates distinct phases of autophagy and autophagosomes.

After understanding how autophagy works in yeast researchers were able to compare yeast to human cells and find similar mechanisms within humans. These mechanisms of autophagy are so similar between yeast and human cells that they are virtually identical. This knowledge, along with scientific advancements, allowed researchers to learn more about autophagy and its effects.

Thanks to the original researchers and those who followed in their footsteps, we have a much better idea of autophagy. We now know that autopsy is an important metabolic function in which cells are broken down and then recycled to be used in a more effective manner. In the process, autophagy is able to provide fuel rapidly and create building blocks for new younger and healthier cells. When we overcome an infection, it is autophagy that can eliminate the remaining bacteria and viruses within our system. When we have damaged organelles and proteins it is autophagy that works as quality control to avoid negative consequences. Autophagy even plays a role in the development of embryos and cellular differentiation.

As you can imagine, with all that autophagy contributes to a malfunctioning autophagy system would be disastrous. It has been found that when autophagy is disrupted it can lead to type II diabetes, Parkinson's disease, Alzheimer's disease, cancer, and much more. For this reason, researchers are attempting to create drugs that can directly target the autophagy system in people with diseases.

However, even if we don't currently have a drug that can directly alter our autophagy system to manage, treat, and prevent diseases, there is still something we can do. While this is a process that happens naturally within a healthy body, with or without our help, it can be accelerated. When we fast we accelerate the metabolism, which also accelerates metabolic autophagy. In fact, during his research in the 1960s, Dr. Ohsumi used fasting of the yeast to induce autophagy.

Therefore, if we regularly practice intermittent fasting we can induce the autophagy response in the same way we increase the human growth hormone and metabolism. This is very likely the reason that fasting has long been shown to decrease aging and increase longevity, as autophagy recycles old cells to make room for young cells.

There are many benefits to inducing autophagy. Not only can we decrease aging, but we can also make use of its other benefits. For instance, can reduce our risk of developing age-related diseases, strengthen our immune system, regulate the inflammation response, right infectious diseases, and even improve our mental health. Autophagy has been directly linked to both depression and schizophrenia, which means that if you are able to enhance your autophagy system you may also, be able to manage your symptoms of illness, whether physical or mental.

When you combine the anti-cancer effects of autophagy, a reduction of glucose (which feeds cancer cells) to starve tumors, and traditional cancer treatments that your doctor prescribes you are likely to greatly increase your chances of successfully eliminating your cancer, or at the very least halting its spread.

Of course, any treatment plan should be discussed with your doctor. Bring up intermittent fasting with your physician so that you can practice it under their care.

Chapter 6: The Types of Fasting, a Systematic Approach

While some types of fasting, such as the 16/8 method, may generally be better than others, everyone is different and therefore may need a different approach. For instance, you may find that the 12/12 method is easier, to begin with, or that you enjoy doing the 16/8 method two days a week and the 12/12 method on the remaining days. Whatever you choose, remember that the priority is to find what works best for your individual circumstances.

However, while there are many different types of fasting methods you can use with intermittent fasting, there are a few guidelines that are important to follow no matter your method. These include:

1. Speak to your doctor. While all doctors may not understand intermittent fasting, it is important to speak to your physician on the matter. This is especially true if you are an adolescent, elderly, chronically ill, pregnant, or breastfeeding. If you are not confident that your doctor has an understanding of the matter don't hesitate to be prepared with studies on the matter! There are many scientific studies online (such as on PubMed) that prove the beneficial effects and safety of intermittent fasting. You can print out a couple of these studies as well as articles on the matter so that your doctor can be informed on the matter and whether or not it is good for your medical condition.

2. Drink enough water. It is important that you stay hydrated and satisfied during your fast, so be sure that you drink plenty of water during this time. However, never drink more than four cups of water within the span of an hour, as the human liver is unable to process more than this in such a short time span. You will also need to be sure to consume electrolytes during your feeding window. Be careful of non-caloric and caffeinated drinks, such as coffee and diet soda, as these can kick your body out of the fasting state.

3. Eat high-quality and healthy foods. Yet, it is possible to practice intermittent fasting without counting calories or changing your diet. However, If you hope to lose weight and gain health it is important to watch what you consume. Not only that, but healthy foods will be more satisfying, whereas junk foods will cause more insulin and blood sugar spikes and crashes, leaving you fatigued and craving more food. Keep in mind that junk foods are designed to be addictive, and these cravings can get in the way of fasting.

Now that you understand the three standard guidelines that should be followed, no matter your fasting method, let's have a more in-depth look at the types of intermittent fasting available.

The 16/8 Method

This type of fast is generally the best option, as it has a high rate of success, isn't overly difficult, and produces many health benefits. If you want to truly master intermittent fasting, then you will want to mater the 16/8 method. For this reason, we will detail exactly how you can follow this method of fasting in a later chapter. However, for the time being, let's have a quick overview of the 16/8 method so that you can easily compare it to the other fasting options available.

For people new to fasting the 16/8 approach may seem extreme. After all, you are limiting yourself only eating for eight hours out of the day! Yet, you will find that this fasting method is much easier to adjust to than you might think. You can easily fit two to three meals into your day, allowing yourself to eat all the nutrients your body requires, leaving you satisfied and energized for the remainder of the day.

Since the fasted state does not begin until twelve hours after eating, shorter fasts (such as the 12/12 fast) do not make the most out of the fasted state. On the other hand, the 16/18 fast allows you to have four whole hours in the fasted state. During these four hours, your metabolism will be accelerated, you will lose more weight, gain more health benefits, and increase beneficial hormone production. If you practice this fast a couple of times a week (or even daily) then you will experience all of the benefits that fasting has to offer.

The 5:2 Method

This method of fasting, also known as the 5:2 "diet" is named such as it allows a person to eat regularly throughout the week and only limit their calorie intake two days of the week. This person may choose to continue to eat however they want, however they will receive the most benefits if they choose to follow a generally healthy lifestyle.

Of course, one of the appeals of this method is that it is flexible and allows a person to still enjoy their favorites without feeling deprived. For instance, you may choose to eat generally healthy, but also allow yourself ice cream or macaroni and cheese over the weekends.

Part of the flexibility of this plan is that you don't have to always practice it on the same days of the week. For instance, one week you may practice your fasting on Monday and Friday, but in another week you might fast on Tuesday and Thursday. Whenever you choose to fast, it is important that you don't do two days back to back. As an example, you don't want to fast on Wednesday and then Thursday. This is because you need to ensure that you are still consuming the proper number of nutrients your body requires, and but fasting in this way two days back to back your body will become weakened. But, by separating fasting days with one or two regular days you can ensure that you are healthy, satisfied, and energized.

While the 5:2 method is known as a type of fast, it is different from the other types of fasts in one major aspect: it is not a full fast. The reason that this method is often referred to as a "diet" is that rather than completely removing food during the fasting period, it only limits the food. A person will typically only eat one-quarter of their usual food intake on these days. This means that women consume an average of five-hundred calories and men an estimated six-hundred.

While there are benefits to the 5:2 method, there are also drawbacks. As the food is not completely removed during the fasting period a person may never reach the fasted state if they eat too frequently. Therefore, avoid any snacking. Instead, eat only one or two meals, within a few hours of each other. By eating two meals in close proximity you can ensure that you are eating in the fasting state, allowing you to receive the benefits of intermittent fasting.

The 24-Hour (Eat-Stop-Eat) Method

This twenty-four hour fast is usually completed once or twice a week. It is a more extreme fasting method, and therefore not for beginners. Although, it can be made easier than it appears. It may seem difficult to wake up in the morning and not eat anything for the entire day until the following morning.

However, just because it is a fast that lasts for a full day doesn't mean you have to go without eating all day. This may seem confusing, but it is really quite simple. Just because the fast lasts for a full day doesn't mean you have to start at the beginning of the day. Instead, many people begin this fast after lunchtime. With this schedule, you can eat breakfast and then have lunch at noon. Begin to fast after lunch and then the following day you can eat a slightly late lunch at 1 pm. This gives you a full 24-hour fast, while still allowing you to get two meals in on each of the two days impacted by your fast. Following this method, you can also choose to begin your fast after breakfast, a snack, or dinner.

While you can have coffee and calorie-free drinks during your fast, you should keep these limited, especially in the beginning. For some people, these drinks may interfere with their fasts. But, if you get accustomed to intermittent fasting and learn to listen to your body, then you will better be able to know whether or not these beverages interfere with the fasting period.

If you are beginning a 24-hour fast for the first time don't feel the need to push yourself too much. First, get accustomed to the 16/8 fast, and then gradually increase the fasting period in one-hour increments. After sixteen hours you can bump it up to seventeen, eighteen, nineteen, and so on.

The Alternate-Day Method

The alternate-day method is one of the most popular options when it comes to scientific studies because it works. With this method, you simply alternate the days you do and don't fast every day. This means if you are fasting on Monday then you don't on Tuesday, then you fast again on Wednesday and don't on Thursday. It continues in this manner, alternating every day.

On this method, women are generally allowed five-hundred calories on fasting days and men six-hundred calories. Try not to spread this calorie consumption out throughout the day, as it will interfere with your fasting period. Instead, try to consume one or two meals with this number of calories relatively close together, so that you go a majority of your day without eating. By doing this, you can maximize the effects of the fasting window.

The alternate-day method is likely the most highly scientifically studied method of fasting, as it is used in a majority of studies on intermittent fasting. You can feel satisfied in knowing that if you choose this approach you will definitely gain success.

One of the reasons that this method of fasting is so popular is because on non-fasting days, a person can eat as they like to a large extent. Obviously, you shouldn't eat only junk food and sweets these days, but you can enjoy treats in moderation. However, be sure that you consume more healthy and real foods than treats, as you want to ensure you are giving your body the nutrients it needs. This means that if you are going to eat cheesecake for dessert you first should eat a healthy dinner.

You also want to avoid limiting your calorie count on non-fasting days, as it would be unhealthy as it would not allow you to properly fuel your body. The alternate-day fasting method should always be practiced with regular calorie consumption on non-fasting days.

The Spontaneous Meal Skipping Method

This is the most popular method for beginners of intermittent fasting, as it allows you to dip your toes into the pool of fasting as it is most convenient. Instead of having a fixed fasting schedule or having to plan ahead you simply go with the flow. If you wake up one day and aren't hungry you can skip breakfast and wait to eat until lunch. Or, if you ate a big breakfast and aren't hungry, then wait to skip lunch and allow breakfast to tide you over until dinnertime.

While this method is generally used when a person finds themselves satisfied and without the need for a meal, sometimes people choose this method for different reasons. For instance, you may be busy and decide to practice a short fast rather than take the time to cook and eat. Or, you may be trying to save money if your budget is tight one week.

However, with this approach, it is important to eat a healthy diet from a day-to-day basis. If you are only skipping the occasional meal, then it won't make much of a difference to your weight alone. On the other hand, if you skip frequent meals you may become malnourished if you don't also focus on eating healthy meals.

Whether you are skipping meals twice a week or daily, with this method you should always pair it with a healthy and balanced diet.

Chapter 7: Common Mistakes and how to Avoid Them

One of the wonderful aspects of intermittent fasting is that it is incredibly easy. In fact, studies have found people regularly enjoy the ease afforded by intermittent fasting that is not available when dieting. Not only is fasting easy, but it is also relatively straight-forward once you are prepared with the knowledge you need. Yet, that does not mean it is impossible to make mistakes. In this chapter, we will be going over the most common mistakes people make, and how you can avoid them. You can use this knowledge to learn from the mistakes of others to gain greater success and experience an easier transition into the lifestyle of fasting.

1. They Don't Keep Busy

Whenever you think about something that you want to do it increases your urge to act on your thoughts. For instance, the more a child thinks about Christmas morning the more likely they are to stay awake to catch a peek of Santa Claus and their presents. The more a person thinks about their crush the more they want to confess their feelings. When a person has a secret, the more they think about the secret the more they want to come right out and say it. The same is true when it comes to fasting. The more you think about wanting to eat the more hungry you will be and the more difficult it will be to restrain yourself.

For this reason, it is better to keep busy so that you don't have time to consider eating. You might have a busy day at work, go shopping, play video games, or enjoy any of your other hobbies. It doesn't matter what you do, but you want to try to stay busy your entire fasting period while you are still in the adjustment phase. Over time, your body will adjust and you will no longer need the distraction, but in the beginning, you should try to keep your mind off of food during your fasting window. This is best done by staying busy with work or fun activities.

2. They Abuse Stimulants

It is okay to have a small amount of coffee or tea when you are fasting. However, it is not a good idea to abuse stimulants while fasting. For instance, if you drink a cup or two to get going in the morning you may feel great then. But, once your next regular mealtime comes around and the caffeine has worn off you will likely be itching for another caffeine fix, resulting in another cup or two.

While it is okay to have two or three cups of coffee or tea throughout the day (without cream or sugar, obviously), it should not become a replacement for food. Try to avoid drinking more than three cups of coffee or tea day to avoid abusing stimulants or becoming overly hooked. You should especially try to avoid caffeine after 4 pm if you go to bed early or 6 pm if you go to bed late.

3. They are Afraid of Hunger

I get it, fasting is a new way of life for most people and change is scary. However, you don't want to allow this fear to get in the way of success. Just because you begin to feel hunger pangs doesn't mean you have to rush to eat right away. The truth is that hunger is a normal and healthy aspect of life. If you allow yourself to feel this hunger for a short time you won't waste away, you won't collapse. You can easily stay healthy and manage a sixteen-hour (or even twenty-four-hour) fast.

In fact, studies have shown that healthy individuals can practice a fast that lasts two to three days without any negative health effects. Obviously, intermittent fasting does not include any fasts longer than twenty-four hours, as otherwise, it would be impossible to maintain on a regular basis while also maintaining adequate nutrition. Yet, with the relatively short fasting windows with intermittent fasting, you can maintain your health despite a bit of hunger.

4. They Think More is Always Better

Just because a twelve, sixteen, or twenty-four hour fast is effective and healthy doesn't mean that more than this is better. Remember, life requires balance. Just because a twenty-four-hour fast two days a week is healthy doesn't mean that a once-weekly forty-eight-hour fast is healthy. This is because by practicing longer fasts on a regular basis you are more likely to develop nutritional deficiencies.

Intermittent fasting utilizes relatively short fasts so that they can be practiced regularly with plenty of nutrition between fasting periods.

While you can practice a twenty-four-hour fast without any caloric intake, you shouldn't do this more than twice a week. Although, if you do want to practice regular long fasting periods, then you can try alternate day fasting. This method is different than the twenty-four hour fast, as it allows you to consume five-hundred calories worth of nutritious food on fasting days.

5. They Make Drastic Changes

You shouldn't jump unto drastic changes too quickly, as you will become overwhelmed, discouraged, hungry, and might even end up quitting and overeating. Instead, allow yourself to slowly dip your toes into changes so that you can adjust with ease.

As an example, if you usually eat every three to four hours then you don't want to jump right into a sixteen-hour fast. Instead, try adopting a twelve-hour fast. This might still seem like a long time, but you can time this fast so that it takes place while you are asleep. For this to be effective you can finish dinner at 7 pm, fast, and then start breakfast at 7 am. If a twelve-hour fast is still too difficult for you then you can try a ten-hour fast.

If you are used to practicing a twelve-hour fast and want to start a sixteen-hour fast you can slowly bump the length of your regular fast an hour or two longer. This will allow you to slowly acclimate, making it require much less effort.

6. They Overeat

It is easy to overeat. After all, you do not have to reduce your caloric intake and you are hungry after a long fast. However, if you eat a lot of high-calorie food quickly after you end your fast, then it is easy to overeat. For instance, you wouldn't want to eat an entire pan of baked macaroni and cheese. Try to stick to reasonable-sized portions of foods. This is especially true of high-calorie foods that add up quickly, such as those that are high in fats.

You can avoid overeating by pairing low-carb vegetables along with all your meals. For instance, if you know you will be eating macaroni and cheese along with some chicken, you can pair it with some steamed broccoli and a nice salad. This way, you won't be tempted to get seconds of the macaroni and cheese.

7. They Eat Poor Quality Meals

Intermittent fasting focuses largely on when and how you eat, not what you are eating. But, this doesn't mean that what you eat doesn't matter. Yes, you can still treat yourself and enjoy some of your favorite foods. But, on average you should be choosing nutrient-dense options. This means you want to eat as few processed or sugary foods as possible. Just because you are practicing fasting doesn't mean that breakfast every day can consist of cake.

You don't have to instantly change your eating habits around, though. You can gradually change what you eat, substituting healthy options for those of poorer quality. It is always a great option to add in more fruits and vegetables, especially though that are low-starch and low-sugar. It is also a good idea to replace refined grains with whole grains, and unhealthy fats with healthy fats. By doing this you can ensure you get all the nutrients your body requires during your eating windows. This will also optimize your weight loss and health benefits.

8. They Give Up too Soon

Intermittent fasting is often rated at easier to follow and maintain than dieting. This isn't only peoples' personal experiences, but the conclusion of researchers who have conducted studies on the matter. Yet, that does not mean it is a perfectly easy method without any bumps along the road. You may still feel hungry from time. While you are adjusting you may get headaches or become worn out.

But, you should keep in mind that these side effects are temporary. Change always takes adjustment, and that includes the change or intermittent fasting. A week or two down the road you will find that the bumps lessen and you have greatly adjusted. Headaches and fatigue will likely go away, hunger will diminish, and you will begin to get used to your new way of life.

Don't give up too soon. Try to allow yourself time to adjust. If you are having a difficult time, then simply try a shorter fasting period and slowly lengthening the fasting window as you feel comfortable.

9. They Eat too Little

While it is easy to overeat when you break your fast, it is also easy to eat too little. This is because fasting affects the hunger hormones, and sometimes you will find yourself full with only a small meal. You want to be careful to ensure that you eat your full recommended daily caloric intake during your eating window. To know what your caloric intake should be you can ask your doctor or find calculators online that use your BMI number to calculate the best option for most people your weight and height.

At the very least, be sure that you never consume fewer than twelve-hundred calories during your eating window.

Chapter 8: Tips and Tricks to Get the Most out of Fasting

Whether you are hoping to lose weight, lower your cholesterol, manage your blood pressure, or reduce your risk of developing age-related diseases, there are many ways that intermittent fasting can help. Just as there are many ways fasting can be effective, there are also many ways in which you can get the most out of your fasting experience and make it an easier one to boot. In the pages of this chapter, you will be provided with a number of tips and tricks that will help you attain the most success possible.

Begin Fasting After Dinner

Whether you are beginning a twelve-hour fast or twenty-four-hour fast, it is often best to start in the evenings, or at least in the late afternoons. This can make it much easier, as you sleep through a majority of your fasting window.

Not only does this allow you to sleep through a majority of the fasting window with shorter fasts, but it also ensures that on twenty-four-hour fasts you can at least get one or two meals in on the day. This will help you to feel more energized and satisfied, helping you to stick with it with less chance of becoming discouraged.

Most people already fast for eight to ten hours a night, so upping that to twelve to sixteen hours is often easily manageable with little to no practice. Just know that it's okay to feel some hunger pangs, as it is a normal aspect of life.

Eat More Satisfying Meals

If you want to not only gain needed nutrition but also stay satisfying throughout your fasting window it is important that you eat filling and satisfying meals. After all, what will keep you full long-term, a doughnut or a bowl of oatmeal with chia seeds and almonds?

You will find that your meals are more satisfying if you combine healthy foods from the three food groups. For instance, the oatmeal option contains whole grains along with both fat and protein. If you choose to eat eggs then you have a good source of protein and fat, so you can add some carbohydrates by adding a side of sweet potato hash or filling an omelet with spinach, avocado, and cilantro.

If you plan to start a fasting window later in the day, then you shouldn't simply have a cup of coffee and a bowl of sugary cereal for breakfast. It is important that you fill your eating windows with better foods, both for your nutrition and so you can stay full and energized during your fasting windows.

If you are used to eating a lot of processed junk foods, it is okay. You can start slowly. Begin by fasting only one or two days a week. This will allow you to eat regularly most of the week and simply focus on filling and nutritious meals on your fasting days. Over time, you can begin to increase the number of healthy foods in your diet so that you are eating well all week long rather than on only a single day.

Drink Plenty of Water

You will find that hunger pangs come sooner or later while you are fasting. While these will be mild for some people, for others they are more difficult. Some people simply feel hunger pangs more strongly or feel more discomfort from even slight hunger pangs.

While you can't avoid hunger pangs altogether, you can help blunt them to help you get through your fast. You can do this by drinking calorie-free options. The best option is always water, as it is good for you and caffeine-free. However, you can also choose to enjoy tea, coffee, and even diet drinks in moderation. It is important to not rely on these other drink options, as you might begin to rely upon them and drink too much of them. However, you are fine with one diet drink a day and two to four cups of tea or coffee.

When trying to blunt your hunger by drinking water, or other liquids, be careful to never drink more than four cups of water (one liter) within the span of an hour. The human liver is unable to safely process more water than this within such a short time-span, making it dangerous to over drink even healthy options.

Breaking Your Fast

You want to avoid breaking your fast with an overly large meal, as this will cause you to overeat. By overeating, you are likely to either consume too many calories or make yourself feel painfully bloated, which nobody wants. Instead, it is best to try to break your fast with a normal-sized meal. Portion yourself out a standard serving of a healthy meal, and don't go back for seconds. If you still want more to eat an hour after you have finished eating, then you can go back for more food.

If you find yourself not hungry and unable to eat a standard meal size, then you can begin with a small snack or appetizer. Enjoy this snack and then wait fifteen minutes to an hour. You will likely find that by eating this snack, your hormones, which have been optimized for maintaining a fast, will readjust themselves for eating normally and you will once again feel hungry and able to eat a regular meal.

Create a Routine

By creating a routine you can make intermittent fasting much easier. This is because the body has a natural circadian rhythm, and the human body naturally likes to stick to its regular rhythm rather than switching things up. This is why fasting can be difficult when you first begin, as it is a rhythm unknown to your body.

You can use this circadian rhythm to your advantage by creating habits and a routine to stick to. This routine can be fostered before you even implement intermittent fasting by creating set times that you go to sleep, wake up, and eat each of your regular meals.

Once you begin to implement fasting you can schedule it around your regular routine. For instance, if you know that you usually go to bed at 11 pm and wake up at 6:30 am you can finish your dinner in the evening at 6:30 pm. This allows you to sleep through most of a twelve-hour fast and eat breakfast first thing in the morning. By using your routine to your advantage in this way you will find that fasting is much simpler.

You can also use your routine to your advantage by always fasting at the same time of day. If you usually fast between 7 pm until 11 am for a sixteen-hour fast then your body will become accustomed to skipping breakfast. Over time, as your circadian rhythm adjusts to this routine you will find that you don't get hungry during this fasting window, making it easy to stick with.

Create a Balanced Mindset

I understand wanting a quick fix, the truth is none of us want to wait around for results. Whether we are attempting to improve our health, lose weight, or increase energy levels, we want to see the results of our hard work soon. But, the problem with this is that it leads to a lot of people to develop feelings of discouragement if they put too much pressure on themselves. They might set goals such as losing five pounds a week, despite it being unhealthy to lose more than two to three pounds of fat (water weight is different) a week. If their cholesterol doesn't lower within two weeks they may feel that there is no point to intermittent fasting, even though they will likely see the results if they waited just a couple weeks longer.

It is important to keep in mind that there are no shortcuts or quick fixes to better health, weight loss, increased energy, and other benefits. Yes, intermittent fasting may be able to provide these results more quickly and reliably than dieting, but that does not mean it will necessarily happen as quickly as you would like.

Allow yourself to create a balanced mindset and goals. Don't expect yourself to see results instantly. Instead, focus on your fasting, eating well, drinking enough water, sleeping properly, caring for your mental health, and exercising for two months. During this time don't worry about results, don't worry, they will come when it is time. If you focus on full mind and body wellness then you are sure to see the results when your body is ready.

Listen to Your Body

If you hope to have a healthy mind and body it is important to listen to the cues your body is telling you. This is not only important for staying healthy, but also for losing weight. After all, if you ignore your body's signs that there is a problem or that it needs something, then it will likely be unable to attain your goals.

When listening to your body, try to pay attention to these cues:

- Energy levels

- Sleepiness

- Sleep quality

- **Athletic abilities**

- **Immune system**

- **Mood fluctuations**

- **Mental health**

- **Hormonal health**

- **Hunger changes**

- **Hydration**

- **Blood work (vitamin levels, minerals, cholesterol, etc.)**

- **Hair and skin health**

- **Weight fluctuations**

Life Situation

Lastly, it is important to consider what is going on in your life. This applies both when you first begin intermittent fasting and as you continue to fast. For instance, you don't want to begin practicing intermittent fasting if you are in the middle of finals, have an exam, or are on a tight deadline for work. It is best to wait until after stressful life events to begin overhauling your lifestyle.

Even if you are accustomed to intermittent fasting, you may want to take a short break during a difficult time. If a family member dies, you are in the middle of the move or are going through any other rough patch you might want to take a break from fasting for a week. It's okay, you can always come back to fasting in a week or two.

It is important to be kind to yourself, don't expect the world from yourself.

Part Two

Chapter 9: The 16/8 Method, an In-depth Look

There are many things to love about the 16/8 method of fasting, which is why is often the fasting method people choose when they want to master intermittent fasting. Firstly, with this method of fasting, you can still enjoy two large or three small meals within your eight-hour eating window. This makes it easy to stay satisfied and nourished, even if you are practicing this fast on a daily basis.

Also sometimes referred to as the Leangains diet, the 16/8 method is also beneficial as it makes use of your fasted state. When a fast only lasts twelve hours or less you do not get to receive nearly all of the benefits intermittent fasting has to offer. This is because your body only finishes the post-absorptive and enters the fasted state twelve hours after eating. The result is that if you are only fasting for twelve hours you are not making use of this valuable opportunity. On the other hand, since this method utilizes a sixteen-hour fast it allows you to stay in the fasted state for several hours. By remaining in the fasted state you will be able to lose weight better, balance your hormones, lower your cholesterol, slow down aging, and much more.

You will find that this method of fasting becomes incredibly easy to implement over time, as it is as simple as skipping one meal a day. If you eat dinner at a reasonable time the night prior and skip breakfast the next morning then congratulations, you have completed a 16/8 fast! Of course, you will have to decide what time exactly you want to finish dinner and start lunch so that you can time them accordingly to ensure that your fast is a full sixteen hours.

While you can complete this fast at any time of the day, most people choose to start it after dinnertime. This is partially because it allows you to sleep through a large portion of your fast. Although, many people often choose this option as they feel less hungry in the morning, therefore making it easy to skip breakfast.

You will find that the 16/8 method can feel the most natural for a large population of people. It fits easily into a person's schedule, to the point that they might not even feel as if they are fasting once they adjust to skipping one meal. If you are worried about how fasting will affect your professional or social life, you will be happy to know that this method can have little to no negative effects on how you get your job done or spending time with friends. Even if you go out drinking with friends past the time you would usually begin your fast in the evening, that just means you can push lunchtime the next day a little later into the afternoon to still allow you a full sixteen hours.

Of course, you can always listen to your body and your individual needs at a time. You aren't required to practice this fast every single day if you want a day or even a week off, that is fine, you are in control! Maybe it's Christmas and you want cinnamon rolls for breakfast or your birthday and you want to enjoy a full day's worth of meals without worrying about eating and fasting windows. This is perfectly fine, as it is your life and you can schedule fasting in a way that leaves you both happy and satisfied.

When you practice the 16/8 fast there is no calorie counting needed, as you are easily reducing your regular caloric intake and making the most of it during your fasted hours. All you have to do is ensure you are eating well during your feeding window. This means you should try to choose healthier options rather than processed foods, fast food, and sugary treats. Even if you have no other choice but to grab fast food you can try to make healthier choices by avoiding fried foods and grabbing something with a lot of vegetables. Chipotle always has a lot of healthy options, but even less expensive fast-food restaurants tend to have some healthy salad choices.

When you are at home try to focus on replacing refined grains with whole grains, sugar with stevia extract or erythritol, trans fats with olive oil or coconut oil, and use a large variety of fruits and vegetables. You will find that if you keep these conditions in mind during your feeding window then you will generally be able to attain your goals. However, if you struggle with the temptation of fried chicken, macaroni and cheese, and ice cream, then you might want to keep a basic calorie count in mind for the day. This does not mean you have to watch every single calorie you eat, but it can help to have a goal in order to avoid the temptation of unhealthy options or going back for seconds in the high-calorie foods rather than in the healthier vegetables. Remember, the purpose of a calorie count (if you even need one) is not to reduce the number of calories you eat within your feeding window; it is only to reduce your risk of overeating the wrong foods. Not everybody needs a calorie count, but some people find it helpful. Do whatever you think is best.

If you choose to use a calorie count as a guideline during your eating window, it is easy to determine what a healthy calorie count should be. You don't have to worry about finding a calorie count for weight loss, just one for maintaining weight. This is because even if you are hoping to lose weight, you will gain this by fasting. The purpose is not to limit yourself during your eating schedule. There are many calculators online that you can use to calculate how many calories you should aim for. These calculators will generally ask your age, gender, height, weight, and activity level. Calculator.Net has one of these calculators under its health and fitness section. If you input your data it will reveal to you the various calorie goal options ranging from maintaining weight to extreme weight loss. If you don't exceed the maintaining weight goal during your eating window then you should be fine.

Before beginning the 16/8 method there are some measures you should set in place. First, you should talk to your doctor. This is an important step, as people with certain medical conditions, the elderly, adolescents, or those who are either pregnant or breastfeeding may not be able to fast. Only a person's doctor will know if fasting is a safe option for this. Remember, while fasting is usually safe, there is always an exception, so you need to be sure that you belong in the majority of people that it is safe for.

When talking with your doctor it is best to explain your reasons for choosing intermittent fasting and reassuring them that you will be consuming the proper number of calories and nutrition during your eating window.

Along with talking with your doctor, you should also decide on a schedule that will work for you. Do you want to go with the normal skipping breakfast, or would you rather skip dinner? What time will you start and end your fast? When deciding on these factors it is important to account for your sleeping times, work schedule, and social calendar.

Lastly, make sure that you have a pantry well-stocked with healthy foods. It may even be helpful to prepare some healthy meals in advance to store in the fridge and freezer. By doing this you can ensure that even if you get too busy to cook you will always have a meal ready when it comes time to break your fast. This will be especially helpful when you first begin intermittent fasting, as your energy might be slightly depleted before it increases. Make sure to take into account the healthy options for all three of the fuel sources: carbohydrates, fat, and protein.

When you first begin fasting don't feel like you have to instantly start with a sixteen-hour fast, even if the 16/8 method is your goal. You can always start out small and work your way toward a longer fasting period. By doing this, you will help yourself not become discouraged from hunger pangs or weakness. Most people will start with an overnight twelve-hour fast. Once they have adjusted to the twelve-hours they will increase the fasting window in one-hour increments, always waiting to become adjusted to the new fasting window before once again upping the fasting window. Before long you will reach your 16/8 goal with little pressure. You will have a hard time believing it can be so easy!

If you find you begin to struggle with hunger pangs during your fasting window you have two options. Either you can cut your fasting window short and start with a shorter window before gradually increasing it or you can try to stick it out. If you decide to stick it out you will find that drinking liquids can greatly help with hunger pangs. Water is generally the best option, but feel free to have coffee and tea in moderation. You may even allow yourself one diet soda a day, although I would recommend having no more than one. Diet sodas (especially those with artificial sweeteners) may throw off your fasting if you drink them in large number.

Lastly, if you are someone who usually exercises you may find that in the beginning, you have to do more gentle workouts. Your body will be attempting to create a new rhythm to accommodate your fasting, and if you push yourself too hard with exercise you will find your body and mind pushed to their limits. By all means, enjoy moderate exercises, but it is probably a good idea to enjoy more intense exercises once you have adjusted.

The beauty of the 16/8 method is that it is incredibly successful without having too many rules or guidelines. If you follow this chapter you should find yourself having success. However, if you still struggle, you can use chapters eight and nine to help you iron out any problems for greater success.

Part Three

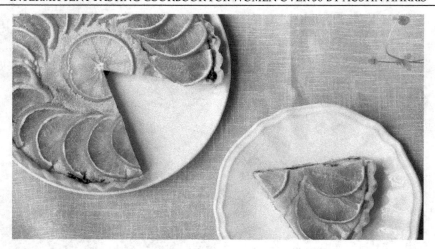

Chapter 10: Twenty-One Day Meal Plan

Whether you skip breakfast or dinner, you will need to choose before you can set a meal plan in stone. While most people choose to skip breakfast, others may not feel hungry at dinnertime or may rely on a breakfast first thing in the morning for strenuous exercise. If this is the case, you can break from the norm and skip dinner, instead. Since skipping breakfast is the more common option, the menu plan in this chapter will reflect that. However, you can always alter this plan to best fit your needs.

This menu plan is also accounting for a person who is on a full 16/8 fasting method. If you decide to go with one of the other methods, such as the 12/12 method, you can easily add in an extra meal. This is simple, as with the 12/12 method a person still eats three meals a day, meaning that for the most part you will eat as normal, with just a little extra time between your dinner the night before and breakfast the next morning.

This menu plan also assumes that you are choosing to follow a standard recommended healthy diet. Of course, it is also possible to follow other eating styles on this plan. For instance, many people choose to combine the ketogenic diet and intermittent fasting. Others may choose to be vegan, vegetarian, gluten-free, dairy-free, or a number of other options. Whatever you choose, know that intermittent fasting is versatile, so you can plan your regular menu plan however you want. Your menu plan does not have to be identical to the one provided within this chapter. If you want to eat a low-carb and high-fat diet, that's fine! It is also perfectly fine to be vegan, gluten-free, or dairy-free. The most important factor is that your menu plan includes balanced and healthy meals. Try to avoid heavily processed or sugary foods to this end.

If you want to make your menu plan more simple make use of canned and frozen vegetables. Sure, fresh options are great, but if the most you can do is steam a bag of broccoli, cauliflower, green beans, or carrots, then that is okay! Yes, you need as big of a variety in fruits and vegetables as possible, but sometimes we need to rely on easier products.

You may also have to account for eating while away from home in your menu plan. If you need to eat a meal at work you will want to prepare a healthy option that you can take with you or be familiar with the healthy menu options of nearby restaurants.

Now that we have covered the basics, let's have a look at a menu plan for the 16/8 fasting method.

Week One

	Breakfast (optional)	Lunch	Dinner
Sunday	Apple Oat Pancakes	Thai Pasta Salad	"Stuffed" Cabbage Casserole
Monday	Whole-Grain Southwestern Toast	BLT Lettuce Wraps	Turkey Sweet Potato Skillet
Tuesday	Scrambled Eggs with Kale and Feta	Whole-Wheat Pasta with Marinara and Meatballs	Steak Tips with Sweet Potatoes, Peppers, and Quinoa
Wednesday	Breakfast Egg Casserole	Chicken Teriyaki Meatball Bowls	Homemade Chicken Strips and Sweet Potato Fries
Thursday	Brown Sugar Peach Oatmeal	Chicken Cranberry Salad Wraps	Tex-Mex Stuffed Poblano Peppers
Friday	Southwestern Omelet	Chicken Zucchini Taquitos	Whole-Wheat Homemade Pizza
Saturday	Butternut Mushroom Hash with Bacon and Eggs	Pork Stir-Fry	Vegetable and Shrimp Skillet with Sausage

Week Two

	Breakfast (optional)	Lunch	Dinner
Sunday	Breakfast Egg Casserole	Chicken Teriyaki Meatball Bowls	"Stuffed" Cabbage Casserole
Monday	Oatmeal with Almond Butter and Chocolate Chips	Whole-Wheat Pasta with Marinara and Meatballs	Black Bean Quesadillas
Tuesday	Chia Seed Chocolate Pudding	Chicken Cranberry Salad Wraps	Vegetarian Chickpea Curry
Wednesday	Whole-Wheat Blueberry Pancakes	Sesame Chicken Slaw	Taco Salad
Thursday	Whole-Grain French Toast	Chicken Pasta Salad with Peas	Turkey Sweet Potato Skillet
Friday	Greek Yogurt with Berries	Avocado Tuna Sandwich on Whole-Grain Bread	Whole-Wheat Caramelized Onion and Avocado Burgers
Saturday	Whole-Grain Southwestern Toast	Whole-Wheat Pesto and Mozzarella Grilled Cheese	Tex-Mex Stuffed Poblano Peppers

Week Three

	Breakfast (optional)	Lunch	Dinner
Sunday	Butternut Mushroom Hash with Bacon and Eggs	Pork Stir-Fry	Steak Tips with Sweet Potatoes, Peppers, and Quinoa
Monday	Oatmeal with Apples	Avocado Tuna Sandwich on Whole-Grain Bread	Whole-Wheat Caramelized Onion and Avocado Burgers
Tuesday	Greek Yogurt with Granola	Chicken Zucchini Taquitos	Vegetable and Shrimp Skillet with Sausage
Wednesday	Breakfast Egg Casserole	Egg Salad and Apple Slices	BBQ Chicken Tostadas
Thursday	Spinach Cheddar Omelet	Whole-Wheat Pesto and Mozzarella Grilled Cheese	Black Bean Quesadillas
Friday	Whole-Grain French Toast	Vietnamese Spring Rolls	Taco Salad
Saturday	Apple Oat Pancakes	Chicken Pasta Salad with Peas	Turkey Sweet Potato Skillet

Chapter 11: Breakfast Recipes

Breakfast is commonly referred to as "the most important meal of the day". However, there are no magical properties exclusive to breakfast that makes it any more important to your day than any other meal. The reason this myth has continued for so long is that traditionally people working labor-intensive jobs require a sustaining meal before heading off to work in the morning and because if you make a bad meal choice for your first meal of the day you are likely to continue making poor meal choices. You can certainly enjoy breakfast instead of dinner if you work a labor-intensive job in the mornings or if you choose to practice strenuous exercise first thing in the morning. Yet, if you are not one of these people then you can likely skip breakfast without any fear.

Even if you do skip breakfast, though, you can still enjoy these recipes for either lunch or dinner!

Butternut Mushroom Hash with Bacon and Eggs

This hash is filling, nutritious, and delicious, all three making it the perfect addition to any feeding window day or night. Sure, it is a traditional breakfast meal, but if you usually skip breakfast why not enjoy "breakfast" for dinner with this hash?

The Details:

The Number of Servings: 1

The Time Needed to Prepare: 5 minutes

The Time Required to Cook: 15 minutes

The Total Preparation/Cook Time: 20 minutes

Number of Calories In Individual Servings: 608

Protein Grams: 31

Fat Grams: 40

Total Carbohydrates Grams: 34

Net Carbohydrates Grams: 28

The Ingredients:

Baby spinach – 1.5 cups

Sea salt

Butternut squash, peeled and cubed – 8 ounces

Button mushrooms, sliced – 4 ounces

Bacon, chopped – 2 slices

Eggs – 2

Black pepper, ground

The Instructions:

- Place the chopped bacon pieces over medium-high heat into a large skillet. While you can certainly use a non-stick skillet, a cast-iron skillet would give this hash a great crispiness, if you have one on hand. Once the bacon is done cooking and reached your desired level of crispiness, you can scoop it out with a spoon and set it aside.

- Add the sliced mushrooms and cubed butternut squash into the bacon fat in the skillet, allowing it to pan-fry while you stir it for approximately ten minutes. You will know that it is ready when the vegetables are browned and the butternut squash is fork-tender.

- Reduce the heat of your vegetable hash to that of medium-low before adding in the spinach and allowing it to wilt for one to ten minutes.

- Once the baby spinach is wilted into the other vegetables add the cooked bacon to the pan as well as enough sea salt and pepper to season the vegetables to your liking.

- Use a spoon and create two egg-sized well in the hash, and then crack one egg into each of the prepared veggie wells. Cover the skillet with a lid and allow it to cook for an additional three to four minutes until the eggs are set. Remove from the heat before enjoying.

Apple Oat Pancakes

These apple and oat pancakes only take a few minutes to whip up, but they are delicious! Of course, you could enjoy these plain, but you can also enjoy them with a moderate amount of maple syrup, honey, baked apples, apple butter, or even whipped cream. Honestly, the toppings are up to you! Feel free to enjoy these alone or with a side of breakfast sausage or an egg for a little added protein.

The Details:

The Number of Servings: 2

The Time Needed to Prepare: 5 minutes

The Time Required to Cook: 15 minutes

The Total Preparation/Cook Time: 20 minutes

Number of Calories In Individual Servings: 303

Protein Grams: 6

Fat Grams: 11

Total Carbohydrates Grams: 45

Net Carbohydrates Grams: 41

The Ingredients:

Apple sauce, sugar-free - .33 cup

Egg – 1

Coconut oil, melted – 1 tablespoon

Honey – 2 tablespoons

Vanilla extract - .5 teaspoon

Oat flour - .5 cup

Baking powder - .5 teaspoon

Cinnamon – .5 teaspoon

Nutmeg - .25 teaspoon

Sea salt – dash

The Instructions:

- Place the apple sauce, honey, sea salt, egg, vanilla extract, and melted coconut oil into a small bowl together and whisk them all together well until fully combined.

- Add the remaining ingredients into the bowl with the wet ingredients and combine them with a whisk or a rubber spatula until there are no clumps remaining. You want to ensure that the baking powder is well-combined without over mixing the batter.

- Grease a large skillet that is coated with a non-stick surface and allow it to preheat before you cook the pancakes over medium heat. You might need to either raise or lower the temperature of the skillet as the pancakes cook.

- Once the pan is hot use a small ladle to measure out four evenly-sized apple oat pancakes. Allow the pancakes to cook until bubbles rise to the surface and then pop and the edges have slightly set. Carefully flip them over and cook for about another minute until cooked through and golden on both sides.

- Remove the pancakes from the heat and serve them with a moderate serving of your favorite healthy toppings.

- **Note:** You can make your own oat flour by simply pulsing some rolled oats in a food processor or blender.

Breakfast Egg Casserole

If you are looking for a protein-packed and low-carb option then look no further! This dish is delicious with breakfast sausage, sweet potato, spinach, and seasonings complementing the eggs, which also serve to boost the protein level to a high number. This is perfect for people who have to exert a lot of energy in the day or who are trying to build strength. Even if you aren't particularly searching for high-protein recipes, you will still love how delicious this healthy option is.

This dish feeds a small crowd, making it great for the whole family. However, it can also be a great meal to make for yourself at the beginning of the week and enjoy a serving of each day without any effort.

The Details:

The Number of Servings: 5

The Time Needed to Prepare: 10 minutes

The Time Required to Cook: 35 minutes

The Total Preparation/Cook Time: 45 minutes

Number of Calories In Individual Servings: 433

Protein Grams: 29

Fat Grams: 30

Total Carbohydrates Grams: 8

Net Carbohydrates Grams: 7

The Ingredients:

Turkey breakfast sausage – 1 pound

Eggs, large – 12

Baby spinach – 1 cup

Sweet potato, small, peeled and thinly sliced – 1

Sea salt - .75 teaspoon

Coconut oil – 1 tablespoon

Black pepper, ground - .125 teaspoon

The Instructions:

- Grease a nine-by-nine inch square baking pan while you allow your oven to preheat to a temperature of Fahrenheit three-hundred and seventy-five degrees. You will want to place the rack of your oven into the center.

- Meanwhile, place the coconut oil and ground turkey breakfast sausage into a large skillet, allowing them to cook until the turkey is completely browned and cooked through without any pink remaining.

- As the turkey browns, you can prepare your vegetables. When you prepare the sweet potato you want to cut it about one-quarter of an inch thick so that it can fully cook while in the oven and become tender. You can either do this with a knife or a mandolin to make it easier to get precise thin slices. Layer these sliced potatoes into the bottom of your prepared pan.

- Using a large bowl whisk together all dozen of the eggs along with the seasonings until the egg and yolk are completely combined. You want to be sure there is no "glop" of egg white separated from the eggs so that they cook evenly and smoothly.

- Add the cooked breakfast sausage over the sliced sweet potatoes and then pour the eggs over the top, lastly topping the pan off with the baby spinach.

- Allow your breakfast egg casserole to cook in the oven until the eggs are firm and starting to brown, about thirty-five to forty minutes. Remove the eggs from the oven and allow the dish to cool for five minutes before slicing and serving.

Whole-Grain Southwestern Toast

This toast is the perfect meal to break your fast with, day or night. It is full of whole-grain bread (homemade is best, but store-bought is fine), avocado, bacon, egg, and salsa. This allows it to be full of nutrition and flavor, keeping you satisfied and happy all day long.

The Details:

The Number of Servings: 1

The Time Needed to Prepare: 5 minutes

The Time Required to Cook: 15 minutes

The Total Preparation/Cook Time: 20 minutes

Number of Calories In Individual Servings: 428

Protein Grams: 15

Fat Grams: 25

Total Carbohydrates Grams: 40

Net Carbohydrates Grams: 29

The Ingredients:

Whole-grain bread, thickly sliced, toasted – 1 slice

Egg – 1

Avocado, pit removed – .5

Cilantro, chopped – 1 tablespoon

Lime juice – 2 teaspoons

Salsa – 2 tablespoons

Sea salt - .25 teaspoon

Bacon, chopped – 1 slice

Red pepper flakes - .25 teaspoon

Cayenne pepper – dash

Black pepper, ground – dash

The Instructions:

- Place the half of an avocado into a bowl and mash it together with the lime juice, chopped cilantro leaves, and seasonings. Set the mixture aside.

- Add the chopped bacon into a large cooking skillet over a temperature of medium-high heat. Once the bacon is cooked and crispy remove it from the pan, setting it aside.

- Begin to toast the bread and add the egg to the skillet along with the bacon fat and allow it to scramble.

- Add the toast to a plate, spread the mashed avocado over the top, add on the scrambled egg and crispy bacon pieces, and then top it off with the prepared salsa. Serve while still warm.

Chapter 12: Lunch Recipes

These lunches are complete meals that you can enjoy any time of the day, whether you are at home or work. If you want, you can even prepare these meals ahead of time to store in the fridge or freezer allowing you to have a week's worth of meals (or more) all ready to enjoy.

Chicken Teriyaki Meatball Bowls

This is a perfect lunch, as it can be served either in a nice bowl at home, or reheated in a plastic container at work. Either way, whether you are eating this lunch at home or at work you will find that the delicious and nutritious meal keeps you satisfied for hours to come. This meal is a great option to make on the weekends and then store in the fridge or freezer for the coming week ahead.

The Details:

The Number of Servings: 3

The Time Needed to Prepare: 10 minutes

The Time Required to Cook: 45 minutes

The Total Preparation/Cook Time: 55 minutes

Number of Calories In Individual Servings: 403

Protein Grams: 37

Fat Grams: 23

Total Carbohydrates Grams: 22

Net Carbohydrates Grams: 17

The Meatball Ingredients:

Chicken, ground – 1 pound

Coconut flour – 2 tablespoons

Green onions, chopped – 2 tablespoons

Sea salt – 1 teaspoon

Ginger, ground – 1 teaspoon

Garlic powder – 1 teaspoon

Coconut oil – 1 tablespoon

Black pepper, ground - .25 teaspoon

The Sauce Ingredients:

Coconut Aminos or tamari sauce - .5 cup

Orange juice – 2 tablespoons

Honey – 2 teaspoons

Arrowroot flour – 1 teaspoon

Sea salt - .5 teaspoon

Garlic powder - .5 teaspoon

Ginger, ground - .25 teaspoon

Black pepper, ground - .25 teaspoon

The Vegetable Ingredients:

Coconut Aminos or tamari sauce – 2 tablespoons

Coconut oil – 1 tablespoon

Sea salt - .5 teaspoon

Water – .25 cup

Broccoli florets – 2 cups

Cauliflower rice – 2.5 cups

The Instructions:

- Begin by preparing the meatballs; you will need to heat up your large cooking oven to a temperature of Fahrenheit three-hundred and seventy-five degrees. You will also need to coat a large cooking sheet with kitchen parchment.

- In a large bowl, combine the meatball ingredients minus the green onions, setting them to the side for later. After you combine the meat mixture divide the meat into evenly-sized portions rolled into balls. You can easily measure out the meatballs if you use a cookie scoop. By the end, you should have about eighteen meatballs.

- Place the prepared meatballs on the prepared cooking sheet lined with kitchen parchment and allow them to cook in the oven until they are fully cooked, about twenty to twenty-five minutes. Using a meat thermometer ensure that the internal temperature of the meatballs is Fahrenheit one-hundred and sixty-five degrees.

- While the meatballs are in the oven begin to prepare the vegetables and sauce. Begin by melting the coconut oil in a large frying pan over a temperature of medium heat and adding in the cauliflower rice, Coconut Aminos, and sea salt. Allow the cauliflower rice to fry on the stove until crispy. Remove the cauliflower rice from the pan and set it aside.

- Into the empty pan that you used for the cauliflower rice, add the broccoli florets, and water. Cover the pan with a lid and allow it to steam until the broccoli is tender. About eight to ten minutes. Remove the excess water from the cooking pan and set the broccoli aside.

- Place all of the sauce ingredients together into a small cooking pan over medium heat, ensuring that you completely whisk in the arrowroot flour so there are no clumps. Allow the sauce to cook until it is hot and thick, about five minutes. Set aside the teriyaki sauce.

- To assemble the serving bowls divide the cauliflower rice between three containers. Toss the broccoli together with two tablespoons of the sauce and then divide it between the containers, as well. Lastly, toss the meatballs into the remaining sauce, divide them between the three containers, and top the meatballs off with the prepared green onions.

- Store these bowls in the fridge for up to four days, or in the freezer for up to four months.

Chicken Pasta Salad with Peas

This pasta salad is made healthy with the addition of whole-wheat pasta and chicken for protein, as well as vegetables. While the peas are delicious in this recipe, if you don't care for peas try substituting them with your favorite vegetable.

The Details:

The Number of Servings: 5

The Time Needed to Prepare: 10 minutes

The Time Required to Cook: 30 minutes

The Total Preparation/Cook Time: 40 minutes

Number of Calories In Individual Servings: 598

Protein Grams: 40

Fat Grams: 17

Total Carbohydrates Grams: 73

Net Carbohydrates Grams: 63

The Ingredients:

Whole-wheat penne pasta, dry – 4 cups

Chicken thighs, boneless, skinless, chopped into bite-sized pieces – 3

Butter – 2 tablespoons

Peas, frozen – 3 cups

Garlic powder - .5 teaspoon

Sea salt - .5 teaspoon

Onion powder - .5 teaspoon

Paprika, smoked - .25 teaspoon

Black pepper, ground - .25 teaspoon

Olive oil – 2 tablespoons

Lemon juice – 5 tablespoons

Parmesan cheese, shredded - .5 cup

Black pepper, ground - .5 teaspoon

Oregano, dried – 1 teaspoon

Onion powder – 1 teaspoon

Garlic powder – 1 teaspoon

Sea salt – 1 teaspoon

The Instructions:

- Place the dried pasta in a pot of salted boiling water and allow it to cook until al dente, according to the instructions on the package. Drain the pasta and run it under cold water to stop the cooking process.

- While the pasta cooks, prepare the chicken thighs. To do this, combine the half teaspoon of garlic powder, half teaspoon of sea salt, half teaspoon of onion powder, quarter teaspoon of smoked paprika, and quarter teaspoon of ground black pepper together in a small bowl.

- Once the spices are combined, rub the spice blend over the chicken pieces until they are evenly coated. Melt the butter in a large cooking pan over a temperature of medium heat and then add in the seasoned chicken, allowing it to cook until cooked through. The chicken is ready once it has an internal temperature of Fahrenheit one-hundred and sixty-five degrees. Set the chicken aside.

- Place the frozen peas into a medium-sized cooking pot full of boiling water, simmering them until fully cooked, about five minutes. Drain the water off from the peas and then add them and the cooked chicken into the pot with the cooked whole-wheat penne pasta.

- Add the olive oil, lemon juice, Parmesan cheese, and remaining spices. Toss all of the ingredients together until they are evenly coated. Divide this mixture between five containers and store in the fridge until ready to enjoy.

Chicken Zucchini Taquitos

Unlike the taquitos you buy in the store, this option is baked and healthy! You can enjoy them on their own, but they are best served with guacamole and salsa for dipping. You can make a single batch to store for the week in the fridge, or you can make a double or triple batch to have a large number stored in the freezer to enjoy as needed.

The Details:

The Number of Servings: 4

The Time Needed to Prepare: 8 minutes

The Time Required to Cook: 27 minutes

The Total Preparation/Cook Time: 35 minutes

Number of Calories In Individual Servings: 464

Protein Grams: 30

Fat Grams: 22

Total Carbohydrates Grams: 38

Net Carbohydrates Grams: 31

The Ingredients:

Corn tortillas, 6-inches – 12

Chicken, ground – 1 pound

Zucchini, medium – 1

Onion, medium, diced - .5

Pepper jack cheese, shredded - .75 cup

Avocado oil – 1 tablespoon

Sea salt - .5 teaspoon, plus a little extra

Chili powder – 3 tablespoons

Cumin, ground – 1 teaspoon

The Instructions:

- Preheat your large oven to a temperature of Fahrenheit four-hundred and twenty-five degrees before lining a large baking sheet with aluminum foil. You will want to grease the aluminum foil with oil or cooking spray.

- Using a kitchen box grater shred the zucchini, using the large holes on the great. Place the shredded zucchini into a clean kitchen towel and squeeze it until it is dry and you have removed a decent amount of liquid. You should be left with a remaining two cups of shredded zucchini.

- Add the avocado oil into a large kitchen skillet over a temperature of medium-high heat along with the ground chicken, grated zucchini, diced onion, and seasonings. Allow all of the ingredients to cook together until the chicken is completely cooked through, with no pink remaining. This should require approximately eight to ten minutes.

- Place the corn tortillas on the baking sheet, spreading them on so that they are covering the entire surface of the pan. They will be overlapping, which is okay. Allow the tortillas to warm in the oven for two minutes, until hot, and then transfer them to a plate covering them with aluminum foil or a pan lid so that they stay hot.

- Remove the tortillas one at a time in order to fill them. To do this, quickly add one-quarter of a cup of the chicken meat in the center of the warm corn tortilla. Sprinkle a tablespoon of the cheese over the top, and then roll the tortilla around the meat mixture so that it is taquito-shaped. Once the taquito is formed transfer it to the prepared baking sheet and continue to prepare the remaining taquitos one-by-one.

- Coat the taquitos with a generous amount of cooking spray, liberally sprinkle salt over the top and allow the taquitos to "fry" in the oven until they are crispy and browned about fifteen to eighteen minutes.

- Remove the taquitos from the oven and serve them with your favorite guacamole, salsa, or cheese sauce.

Chapter 13: Dinner Recipes

These dinner recipes can be enjoyed day or night, after all, there is no reason that you can't enjoy a deliciously savory meal for breakfast. Enjoy these dishes alone, with family, or friends. Either way, you will find that you can enjoy delicious meals while still losing weight and gaining health.

Black Bean Quesadillas

These black bean quesadillas are vegetarian, yet still full of protein! You will love the sweet and savory flavor they have, along with the creaminess provided from the avocado. Enjoy these quesadillas alone or with friends.

The Details:

The Number of Servings: 4

The Time Needed to Prepare: 10 minutes

The Time Required to Cook: 20 minutes

The Total Preparation/Cook Time: 30 minutes

Number of Calories In Individual Servings: 439

Protein Grams: 14

Fat Grams: 25

Total Carbohydrates Grams: 39

Net Carbohydrates Grams: 28

The Ingredients:

Avocados, mashed – 1

Sweet potato, large – 1

Whole-wheat tortillas, large – 4

Black beans, canned, drained, rinsed - .5 cup

Corn, canned, drained, rinsed - .25 cup

Jalapeno, diced – 1 teaspoon

Cilantro, chopped – 2 tablespoon

Orange sweet pepper, mini – 1

Red sweet pepper, mini – 1

Cheddar cheese, shredded – 1 cup

Taco seasoning – 1 tablespoon

Butter, softened – 1 tablespoon

Olive oil – 2 teaspoons

The Instructions:

- Using a fork poke several holes into the sweet potato before rubbing down the entire surface with one teaspoon of the olive oil. Wrap the oil-coated sweet potato in paper towels and microwave it until it is very tender. About eight minutes. You can also use sweet potatoes that were cooked in the oven or pressure cooker if you want.

- Meanwhile, slice the sweet peppers and jalapeno in half, removing the seeds before dicing the peppers. Add the peppers to a large skillet on the stove and allow them to cook with the remaining teaspoon of olive oil on the stove for five minutes until they have become tender. Add the corn, black beans, and taco seasoning, stirring all of the ingredients together until well-combined. Allow this mixture to cook together for three minutes until the beans are hot, and then set it aside.

- Lay out your four tortillas. On one side of each tortilla you will want to spread the softened butter, then flip them over and use the other side for the filling. Over the top of each tortilla spread approximately three tablespoons of the soft sweet potato. Afterward, spread the mashed avocado over the top of each tortilla.

- Add one-quarter of a cup of the black bean mixture to each tortilla, divide the shredded cheese between them, and then divide the cilantro between them. Fold each tortilla in half so that the filling is covered and the butter is facing outward.

- Place a quesadilla in a skillet pan over a temperature of medium heat and allow it to cook until the bottom side is browned. Flip the quesadilla over and continue to cook until the opposite side is browned, as well. Remove the quesadilla from the stove and continue to cook the remaining three.

- Slice the quesadillas and serve them immediately while still warm.

Vegetarian Chickpea Curry

This chickpea is full of fiber and nutrients, which will keep you full all day long. While cooked brown rice is used in the recipe, you can always serve it with other cooked whole grains and seeds, such as wheat berries, quinoa, or millet. As this recipe uses canned beans it is incredibly easy to cook, making it a great option for a last-minute quick meal.

The Details:

The Number of Servings: 4

The Time Needed to Prepare: 5 minutes

The Time Required to Cook: 20 minutes

The Total Preparation/Cook Time: 25 minutes

Number of Calories In Individual Servings: 548

Protein Grams: 11

Fat Grams: 28

Total Carbohydrates Grams: 66

Net Carbohydrates Grams: 54

The Ingredients:

Chickpeas, canned, drained – 15 ounces

Coconut milk, canned, full-fat – 13.5 ounces

Tomatoes, canned, crushed – 15 ounces

Onion, large, diced – 1

Curry powder – 1 tablespoon

Garam masala – 2 teaspoons

Garlic, minced – 4 cloves

Olive oil – 2 teaspoons

Cayenne pepper – dash

Sea salt – 1 teaspoon

Lime juice – 3 tablespoons

Maple syrup – 2 teaspoons

Cilantro, chopped - .25 cup

Brown rice, cooked – 3 cups

The Instructions:

- Place the olive oil in a large skillet and then add in the diced onions, allowing them to sauté over medium heat for five minutes until they become transparent. Add in the garlic and allow it to cook for an additional minute so that the garlic releases its flavors but does not burn.

- Add the spices to the onion and garlic mixture, cooking them over the heat for one to two minutes, until they are also fragrant.

- Into the onion and spice mixture add the crushed tomatoes and drained chickpeas, allowing all of the ingredients to come to a simmer and cook for five minutes. Add in the sea salt, coconut milk, and maple syrup before allowing the ingredients to cook for five more minutes.

- Remove the curry from the heat, stir in the lime juice and cilantro, and serve it over the cooked brown rice.

Tex-Mex Stuffed Poblano Peppers

Whether you are looking for a low-carb meal or not, you will love these stuffed peppers that have only seven net carbs. You will also find that these keep you full and energized all day, as they contain over thirty grams of protein!

The Details:

The Number of Servings: 4

The Time Needed to Prepare: 20 minutes

The Time Required to Cook: 30 minutes

The Total Preparation/Cook Time: 50 minutes

Number of Calories In Individual Servings: 353

Protein Grams: 33

Fat Grams: 20

Total Carbohydrates Grams: 8

Net Carbohydrates Grams: 7

The Ingredients:

Poblano peppers, medium – 4

Onion, medium, diced - .5

Tomatoes, medium, diced – 2

Olive oil – 4 teaspoons

Cumin, ground – 1 teaspoon

Garlic, minced – 4 cloves

Oregano, dried – 1 teaspoon

Cilantro, fresh, chopped - .5 cup

Sea salt – 1 teaspoon

Colby Jack cheese, shredded – 1.5 cups

Chicken breast, cooked, shredded – 2 cups

The Instructions:

- Preheat your oven to a temperature of Fahrenheit four-hundred degrees and prepare a baking sheet by greasing it with one teaspoon of the oil.

- While the oven preheats begin to prepare the peppers. To do this wash and dry the peppers, slice the tops off and remove the seeds. Cut a slit into one side of each pepper.

- Add the remaining three teaspoons (one tablespoon) of olive oil into a large skillet on the stove over a temperature of medium-high heat. Into the skillet add the garlic, onion, tomatoes, sea salt, oregano, and cumin. Allow these to cook together until the liquid evaporates, about seven minutes.

- Remove the skillet from the heat and stir in the shredded Colby Jack, chopped cilantro, and shredded cooked chicken.

- Stuff the peppers with the prepared chicken and vegetable filling, pressing it deep into the pepper so that it fills the entire cavity. Once stuffed, place the peppers on the prepared greased baking sheet with the slit side facing upward. Continue to cook until the poblanos are soft and begin to char.

- Remove the peppers from the oven, allow them to rest for five minutes, and then serve.

"Stuffed" Cabbage Casserole

Stuffed cabbage doesn't have to be a difficult and time-consuming dish. With this recipe, you can get all the flavor and health benefits of stuffed cabbage but in a quick and easy to make a casserole! Enjoy this dish in only twenty-five minutes on the stove, or you can prepare it in a slow cooker for a meal ready in a few hours.

The Details:

The Number of Servings: 5

The Time Needed to Prepare: 5 minutes

The Time Required to Cook: 20 minutes

The Total Preparation/Cook Time: 25 minutes

Number of Calories In Individual Servings: 539

Protein Grams: 31

Fat Grams: 37

Total Carbohydrates Grams: 21

Net Carbohydrates Grams: 16

The Ingredients:

Ground beef, 15/15%– 1 pound

Onion, large, diced – 1

Fire-roasted tomatoes, canned – 14 ounces

Bell pepper, seeds removed, diced – 1

Olive oil – 3 tablespoons

Garlic, minced – 4 cloves

Paprika, smoked - .5 teaspoon

Garlic powder - .5 teaspoon

Sea salt – 1 teaspoon

Oregano, dried - .5 teaspoon

Onion powder - .5 teaspoon

Cabbage, small head, chopped – 1

Cheddar cheese, shredded – 2 cups

The Instructions:

- In a large pan on the stove cook the beef with the olive oil, diced onion, and diced bell pepper over a temperature of medium-high. Allow this to cook until the beef is fully cooked with no pink remaining. Add in the minced garlic and cook for an additional two minutes.

- Stir the fire-roasted tomatoes and spices into the large pan and then top it off with the chopped cabbage. Cover the pan with a lid and allow the cabbage to cook until tender, about fifteen to twenty minutes.

- Stir the ingredients in the pot together then sprinkle the cheese over the top. Cover the pot with the lid once again until the cheese is melted, and then serve.

Vegetable and Shrimp Skillet with Sausage

This vegetable skillet is full of shrimp and pork sausage, which is perfect when you want a protein or fat boost. You will find that this dish contains a variety of vegetables, making it a great way to get a variety of nutrients. This dish is easily enjoyed immediately, or you can prepare it in advance and store it in the fridge or freezer until a later date.

The Details:

The Number of Servings: 4

The Time Needed to Prepare: 5 minutes

The Time Required to Cook: 10 minutes

The Total Preparation/Cook Time: 15 minutes

Number of Calories In Individual Servings: 573

Protein Grams: 41

Fat Grams: 35

Total Carbohydrates Grams: 24

Net Carbohydrates Grams: 19

The Ingredients:

Zucchini squash, medium – 2

Yellow summer squash, medium – 2

Bell pepper – 2

Asparagus – 1.5 pounds

Shrimp, large, peeled and deveined – 1 pound

Pork sausage – 14 ounces

Sea salt - .5 teaspoon

Olive oil – 2 tablespoons

Cajun seasoning – 2 tablespoons

Black pepper, ground - .25 teaspoon

The Instructions:

- Slice the zucchini and summer squash into slices one-quarter of an inch thick each. Slice the bell peppers into strips and the asparagus spears into bite-sized pieces. You will also want to slice the pork sausage into rounds.

- Place all of the ingredients into a large skillet together, tossing them together to coat them in the seasonings and oil. Allow the skillet dish to cook over a temperature of medium-high heat until the shrimp is fully cooked and pink, about five to seven minutes. The vegetables should be fork-tender.

- Serve up the dish immediately or store it in a container to enjoy on another day.

Steak Tips with Sweet Potatoes, Peppers, and Quinoa

These steak tips are full of flavor, which is perfectly accented by the vegetables, quinoa, and tamari sauce. This dish is best served immediately and can be enjoyed with family and friends.

The Details:

The Number of Servings: 5

The Time Needed to Prepare: 15 minutes

The Time Required to Cook: 30 minutes

The Total Preparation/Cook Time: 45 minutes

Number of Calories In Individual Servings: 393

Protein Grams: 30

Fat Grams: 19

Total Carbohydrates Grams: 26

Net Carbohydrates Grams: 22

The Ingredients:

Flat iron steak, cut into one-inch pieces – 1 pound

Sweet potato, medium, sliced into one-inch pieces – 1

Bell peppers, sliced into one-inch pieces – 2

Garlic, minced – 3 cloves

Sea salt – 1.5 teaspoon

Olive oil – 3 tablespoons

Green onions, thinly sliced – 4

Cilantro, fresh, chopped -2 tablespoons

Tamari sauce – 2 tablespoons

Black pepper, ground – 2 teaspoons

Quinoa, cooked – 2 cups

The Instructions:

- Place the diced sweet potato and half teaspoon of the sea salt into a glass and microwave-safe bowl. Cover this bowl with a glass plate and microwave it for five to six minutes, until it becomes tender. Halfway through the cooking process stir the sweet potatoes around to ensure even cooking. The sweet potatoes are ready when they are fork-tender, but you want a slight bit of firmness remaining so that they do not fall apart after cooking further on the stove.

- Into a large skillet heat two tablespoons of the olive oil before adding in the cut steak. Try to place the steak in a single layer so that it is not overlapping. Allow it to cook, turning the pieces over every two minutes until the outside is seared and the center is medium or medium-rare. This should take about ten minutes over medium heat. Remove the steak from the skillet immediately and set it aside.

- Add the remaining tablespoon of the olive oil to the now-empty skillet along with the sweet potato. Toss the sweet potatoes until they are fully coated in the oil and then allow them to brown in the skillet, taking about three to four minutes.

- Into the skillet add the garlic, cooking for one minute. Add in the bell peppers and sauté until they are tender. About four minutes.

- Add the steak back to the skillet, along with the tamari sauce. Toss the ingredients together and cook until all the liquid is evaporated. About one to two minutes. Add the remaining sea salt, cooked quinoa, chopped cilantro, and ground black pepper. Serve immediately.

Turkey Sweet Potato Skillet

This hash is quick and easy to make, but full of nutrients. Sweet potatoes have frequently been referred to as "the healthiest vegetable in the produce department" for good reason. With this recipe, you can make use of the many nutrients found not only within sweet potatoes but also within the turkey and spices.

The Details:

The Number of Servings: 4

The Time Needed to Prepare: 5 minutes

The Time Required to Cook: 25 minutes

The Total Preparation/Cook Time: 30 minutes

Number of Calories In Individual Servings: 391

Protein Grams: 30

Fat Grams: 16

Total Carbohydrates Grams: 32

Net Carbohydrates Grams: 27

The Ingredients:

Turkey, ground – 1 pound

Onion, diced – 1

Bell pepper, diced – 1

Water - .5 cup

Sweet potatoes, peeled and diced – 3

Mozzarella, shredded - .5 cup

Black pepper, ground - .25 teaspoon

Cilantro, fresh, chopped - .25 cup

Garlic, minced – 3 tablespoons

Cumin, ground – 1.5 tablespoons

Olive oil – 2 tablespoon

Sea salt - .5 teaspoon

Chili powder – 1 teaspoon

The Instructions:

- Add the olive oil and garlic to a large skillet that is set to a heat of medium-high, allowing the garlic to cook for one minute before you add in the ground turkey. Cook the turkey, stirring it occasionally, until it is cooked through completely, approximately eight minutes.

- Add the spices, bell pepper, and onion to the skillet, cooking them for four minutes. Add in the water and sweet potato before covering the skillet with a lid, allowing it to cook for six to eight minutes until the sweet potato is fork-tender. If the skillet runs out of water before the sweet potatoes are done cooking simply add a little more water.

- Remove the lid from the skillet and sprinkle the shredded mozzarella over the top, giving it a few minutes to melt. Once melted, top the skillet with the fresh chopped cilantro and serve.

Chapter 14: Snack Recipes

One of the great things about intermittent fasting is that it reduces your need to snack. You are able to be satisfied with complete meals during your eating windows and don't eat anything during your fasting period. However, sometimes you might find yourself in the middle of an eating window without a meal ready to eat. If that is the case, you can rely on these quick and easy snacks to see you through. Not only are they easy to make, they are also delicious!

Yogurt Berry Bark

This yogurt bark is incredibly simple and quick to whip up, but it is full of flavor. The sweet honey perfectly accents the Greek yogurt, and the creaminess of the yogurt pairs wonderfully with the mixed berries and chocolate chips. Keep this bark on hand so that you always have a quick and easy snack prepared.

The Details:

The Number of Servings: 5

The Time Needed to Prepare: 7 minutes

The Time Required to Cook: 0 minutes

The Total Preparation/Cook Time: 7 minutes

Number of Calories In Individual Servings: 267

Protein Grams: 18

Fat Grams: 5

Total Carbohydrates Grams: 36

Net Carbohydrates Grams: 33

The Ingredients:

Greek yogurt, plain, non-fat – 3 cups
Honey - .33 cup

Vanilla – 1 teaspoon

Chocolate chips, mini - .33 cup

Blueberries – 1 cup

Raspberries - .5 cup

Strawberries, sliced - .5 cup

The Instructions:

- Line a cooking sheet with kitchen parchment to prevent sticking and set it aside.

- In a small bowl whisk together the honey, vanilla, and plain Greek yogurt. Once well combined spread this mixture out in a thin layer onto the parchment. You want it thin, but not overly thin, or else it will crack. Try to get the layer about one-quarter of an inch thick.

- Sprinkle the blueberries, raspberries, sliced strawberries, and chocolate chips evenly over the top of the yogurt mixture. If you want, you can even drizzle extra honey over the top of the bark at this point.

- Place the baking sheet with the yogurt bark in the freezer, allowing it to chill for at least three hours, but ideally eight. Once it has frozen completely you can peel the bark off of the parchment paper and then break it into pieces to enjoy.

- Store the bark in the freezer in a plastic container for up to a month.

Garlic Sweet Potato Fries

These garlic sweet potato fries are quite addicting, and the perfect snack! However, you can also enjoy them as a side dish to nearly any meal. These will especially complement healthy hamburgers, which you can serve with or without a bun. Enjoy these fries plain, or dip them in garlic aioli.

The Details:

The Number of Servings: 2

The Time Needed to Prepare: 10 minutes

The Time Required to Cook: 25 minutes

The Total Preparation/Cook Time: 35 minutes

Number of Calories In Individual Servings: 173

Protein Grams: 2

Fat Grams: 6

Total Carbohydrates Grams: 26

Net Carbohydrates Grams: 22

The Ingredients:

Sweet potatoes, medium, peeled – 2

Sea salt - .25 teaspoon

Garlic powder - .125 teaspoon

Paprika - .125 teaspoon

Olive oil – 1 tablespoon

Black pepper, ground - .125 teaspoon

The Instructions:

- Preheat your oven to a temperature of four-hundred and fifteen degrees Fahrenheit and then line a cooking sheet with kitchen parchment.

- Slice the sweet potatoes into wedges about one-quarter of an inch thick. If you have a vegetable spiralizer you can also make curly fries.

- Place the prepared fries in a bowl and toss it together with the olive oil and seasonings, and then lay them out on the baking sheet in a single layer. Try to make the fries overlap as little as possible. Cook the fries for fifteen minutes, stir them around on the pan, and then cook for an additional fifteen minutes until crispy. Serve the sweet potato fries while still hot.

Peanut Butter Chocolate Chip Bars

Whether you are at home or on the go, these snack bars are the perfect treat! You can easily store these in the fridge or your car to have a delicious snack at a moment's notice.

The Details:

The Number of Servings: 6

The Time Needed to Prepare: 5 minutes

The Time Required to Cook: 0 minutes

The Total Preparation/Cook Time: 5 minutes

Number of Calories In Individual Servings: 184

Protein Grams: 3

Fat Grams: 10

Total Carbohydrates Grams: 21

Net Carbohydrates Grams: 19

The Ingredients:

Peanut butter, natural, sugar-free - .25 cup

Banana, mashed - .5 cup

Coconut flour, sifted - .66 cup

Honey - .25 cup

Chocolate chips, mini – 2 tablespoons

Vanilla extract - .5 teaspoon

The Instructions:

- Line an eight-by-four inch loaf pan with parchment paper and set it aside.

- In a medium-sized bowl for the purpose of mixing mix together the mashed banana, creamy natural peanut butter, honey, and vanilla extract. Once it is creamy stir in the coconut flour and the chocolate chips until the mixture is well combined.

- Using a spoon or spatula spread the mixture into the bottom of the loaf pan. Using either the spatula or your hands, press down the mixture until it is pressed firmly and evenly over the entire pan. Place the pan in the refrigerator, allowing it to chill for one to two hours.

- Pick up the kitchen parchment from the edges of the loaf pan after the bars have chilled. Lift the mixture out of the loaf pan and then cut it into six evenly-sized bars. Place the bars in a plastic container in the fridge or freezer.

- When taking these bars on-the-go be sure to place them in a cold bag along with an ice pack.

Crispy Edamame

This crispy edamame is a wonderful snack full of nutrients and protein, complemented by healthy fats from olive oil. Edamame doesn't only taste amazing, but they also have some amazing health benefits, as studies have shown that people who eat soy on a regular basis are much less likely to develop certain types of cancer.

The Details:

The Number of Servings: 3

The Time Needed to Prepare: 5 minutes

The Time Required to Cook: 15 minutes

The Total Preparation/Cook Time: 20 minutes

Number of Calories In Individual Servings: 228

Protein Grams: 17

Fat Grams: 13

Total Carbohydrates Grams: 14

Net Carbohydrates Grams: 7

The Ingredients:

Edamame, frozen, shelled – 1 pound

Olive oil – 1 tablespoon

Parmesan cheese, shredded – 3 tablespoons

Sea salt - .5 teaspoon

Red pepper flakes - .25 teaspoon

Garlic powder - .25 teaspoon

Black pepper, ground - .125 teaspoon

The Instructions:

- Preheat your oven to a temperature of Fahrenheit four-hundred degrees and prepare a cooking sheet by lining it with kitchen parchment.

- Place the frozen and shelled edamame on the lined baking sheet and drizzle the olive oil over it. Add the seasonings and shredded Parmesan cheese over the top and then toss the ingredients all together. Be sure that the edamame is evenly coated in the seasonings.

- Set the pan of edamame in the oven and allow them to bake until crispy, about fifteen minutes. Once crispy, remove the edamame from the oven and serve immediately.

Baked Plantain Chips

Plantain chips are a delicious side dish in many cuisines, but being deep-fried they aren't always the healthiest choice. However, these plantain chips are oven-fried, making them a much better option! Enjoy these alone as a snack or as a side dish your favorite meals.

The Details:

The Number of Servings: 1

The Time Needed to Prepare: 5 minutes

The Time Required to Cook: 15 minutes

The Total Preparation/Cook Time: 20 minutes

Number of Calories In Individual Servings: 278

Protein Grams: 2

Fat Grams: 7

Total Carbohydrates Grams: 57

Net Carbohydrates Grams: 53

The Ingredients:

Plantain, green – 1

Sea salt – to taste

Olive oil - .5 tablespoon

The Instructions:

- Preheat your oven to a temperature of Fahrenheit three-hundred and fifty degrees and line a cooking sheet with kitchen parchment.

- Using a small knife slice through the peel of the plantain and then remove the fruit whole from the peel. This is needed, as the peel of plantain is much tougher than that of a banana.

- Using a mandolin on its most thin setting slice the plantain chips evenly. If you don't have a mandolin slice it as thin as possible with a knife. Toss the sliced plantain pieces with the olive oil.

- Place the plantain slices on the prepared kitchen parchment in a single layer so that they do not overlap. Sprinkle them with sea salt and then allow them to bake until golden around the edges, about fifteen to twenty minutes.

- Remove the chips from the oven, allow them to cool for five minutes to crisp up more, and serve.

Chapter 15: Dessert Recipes

While you can certainly enjoy desserts when intermittent fasting, try to not partake of them on a daily basis if you are trying to lose weight. For those watching their waistline, it is probably best to enjoy desserts no more than two or three times a week. When you do choose to enjoy desserts, while you can certainly treat yourself to something special on occasion, you will be happy to know that the recipes in this chapter are healthier than most desserts available, allowing you to indulge and watch your health simultaneously.

Chocolate Crispy Bars

Unlike the crispy rice bars you can buy at the store, these are much healthier! These cut down on the sugar content greatly by using a small amount of agave syrup, reduce the refined carbohydrates by using puffed quinoa instead of white rice, and uses homemade coconut oil "chocolate" full of healthy fats.

The Details:

The Number of Servings: 6

The Time Needed to Prepare: 5 minutes

The Time Required to Cook: 0 minutes

The Total Preparation/Cook Time: 5 minutes

Number of Calories In Individual Servings: 172

Protein Grams: 2

Fat Grams: 10

Total Carbohydrates Grams: 19

Net Carbohydrates Grams: 17

The Ingredients:

Puffed quinoa – 1.5 cups

Cocoa powdered - .25

Coconut oil, melted - .5

Agave syrup - .25 cup

Vanilla extract – 1 teaspoon

Sea salt – dash

The Instructions:

- Line a cooking sheet with kitchen parchment and then set it aside.

- In a bowl whisk together the cocoa powder, melted coconut oil, agave syrup, vanilla extract, and sea salt until it becomes completely smooth with no clumps. Fold in the puffed quinoa until it is evenly distributed.

- Using a spoon make six piles of the chocolate quinoa mixture on the prepared parchment. Try to get the six piles of chocolate approximately the same size; it might help you to use a scoop.

- Slightly press down the mounds so that they are round cookie shapes and then set the cooking sheet in the freezer to chill for one hour. After the hour has passed remove the chocolate from the cooking sheet, place them in a container, and store the chocolate in the fridge.

Gooey Zucchini Brownies

Just because these brownies are grain-free and much healthier than the alternative options doesn't mean that they aren't as delicious. These gooey brownies taste amazing and are given a perfectly moist texture thanks to the zucchini. You will come to love these brownies in no time! Make them as the recipe details, or try adding nuts, if you would like.

The Details:

The Number of Servings: 6

The Time Needed to Prepare: 10 minutes

The Time Required to Cook: 35 minutes

The Total Preparation/Cook Time: 45 minutes

Number of Calories In Individual Servings: 343

Protein Grams: 6

Fat Grams: 23

Total Carbohydrates Grams: 33

Net Carbohydrates Grams: 28

The Ingredients:

Coconut flour – 2 tablespoons

Cocoa powder - .5 cup

Sea salt - .5 teaspoon

Baking soda - .5 teaspoon

Coconut oil, melted – 2 tablespoons

Egg, large – 1

Maple syrup - .25 cup

Tahini paste - .5 cup

Coconut sugar - .5 cup

Vanilla extract – 1 teaspoon

Zucchini, squeezed of excess moisture, shredded – 1 cup

Chocolate chips - .33 cup

The Instructions:

- Preheat the oven to a temperature of Fahrenheit three-hundred and fifty degrees and prepare an eight-by-eight inch baking pan by lining it with kitchen parchment and greasing it with cooking spray.

- Make sure that your zucchini has had the excess moisture removed. You can do this by placing it in a clean kitchen towel or paper towel and pressing it until you have removed as much liquid as possible. This is very important; get as much water out as you can.

- Place the zucchini that you have removed the moisture from into a bowl along with the egg, maple syrup, coconut sugar, tahini paste, and vanilla extract. Stir all of the ingredients together until well-combined. Add in the cocoa powder, mixing until combined.

- Into the bowl with the zucchini and cocoa add the baking soda, coconut flour, sea salt, and melted coconut oil. Stir until all of the ingredients are incorporated, and then gently fold in the chocolate chips.

- Pour the brownie batter into the prepared pan and then place it in the center of the oven to cook for thirty to thirty-five minutes, until a toothpick you place in the middle of the pan is removed clean with only a few crumbs attached. You don't want the mixture to be completely wet, but a slightly gooey texture is okay.

- Allow the brownies to cool completely before slicing and serving. You don't want to cut them before they are completely cooled, as they will fall apart if sliced too soon.

Cinnamon Apple Crisp

This warm apple crisp is simple yet delicious. Enjoy it on its own or with a dollop of either Greek yogurt or whipped cream. Whether you are enjoying this as a special Sunday morning treat or a dessert next to an autumn bonfire, you are sure to love how delicious it turns out.

The Details:

The Number of Servings: 6

The Time Needed to Prepare: 5 minutes

The Time Required to Cook: 15 minutes

The Total Preparation/Cook Time: 20 minutes

Number of Calories In Individual Servings: 370

Protein Grams: 4

Fat Grams: 14

Total Carbohydrates Grams: 59

Net Carbohydrates Grams: 54

The Ingredients:

Whole-wheat flour - .33 cup

Rolled oats - .5 cup

Pecans, chopped - .5 cup

Dark brown sugar - .33 cup

Sea salt - .25 teaspoon

Cinnamon - .25 teaspoon

Butter, cold, sliced into small cubes - .25 cup

Green apples, medium, peeled – 6

Cinnamon – 1 teaspoon

Maple syrup - .33 cup

Vanilla extract – 1 teaspoon

Nutmeg - .125 teaspoon

The Instructions:

- Preheat the oven to a temperature of Fahrenheit three-hundred and fifty degrees before greasing an eight-by-eight inch baking dish, setting it aside.

- Begin by making the topping. In order to do this, you need to combine the whole-wheat flour, rolled oats, cinnamon, dark brown sugar, and chopped almonds in a medium-sized kitchen bowl. Add in the cold butter, combining it in your hands until it forms a crumbly dough that resembles sand. You want some clumps of butter, but nothing too big. Although, if you have a pastry cutter you can use one of these instead of your hands.

- Place the whole-wheat oat topping mixture in the fridge to chill while you prepare the remainder of the crisp.

- After peeling the apples slice them into pieces about one-quarter to one-half of an inch thick. Toss the sliced apples together with the vanilla extract, maple syrup, nutmeg, and cinnamon in a clean medium-sized bowl for the purpose of mixing. Set this mixture aside and allow it to rest for five to ten minutes.

- After the apple mixture has sat for a few minutes add one-third of a cup of the crumble mixture into the apples, tossing them together. Pour the apple mixture into the prepared baking dish and then sprinkle the remaining oat topping over the top of it.

- Place the crisp in the oven on top of a baking sheet to prevent it from bubbling over and burning in the bottom of the oven. Bake until the apples are tender, the topping is golden, and the filling is bubbling. It should require forty-five to fifty-five minutes in the oven.

- Remove the apple crisp from the oven, allowing it to cool for ten minutes before serving. Enjoy alone or with a dollop of either Greek yogurt or whipped cream.

Chocolate Chip Cookie Dough

Enjoy this cookie dough by the spoonful! While traditional contains eggs, which run the risk of causing salmonella poisoning, this cookie dough does not contain eggs. This dough is meant to be enjoyed by the spoonful, rather than baked.

The Details:

The Number of Servings: 5

The Time Needed to Prepare: 5 minutes

The Time Required to Cook: 0 minutes

The Total Preparation/Cook Time: 5 minutes

Number of Calories In Individual Servings: 244

Protein Grams: 2

Fat Grams: 8

Total Carbohydrates Grams: 40

Net Carbohydrates Grams: 39

The Ingredients:

Milk – 2 tablespoons

Butter, softened – 2 tablespoons

Brown sugar – .5 cup

Sugar – 2 tablespoons

Flour, all-purpose – .5 cup

Vanilla extract – .5 teaspoon

Chocolate chips, mini - .25 cup

The Instructions:

- Using a whisk cream together the butter and brown sugar in a small bowl until it is creamy and smooth. Whisk in the milk and vanilla extract until fully combined.

- Stir the flour, sugar, and mini chocolate chips into the bowl with the sugar and butter until the mixture is evenly combined.

- Enjoy the batter right away or chill it in the fridge to enjoy later. You can even freeze this dough in serving-size portions so that you always have a sweet treat ready in the freezer, it will only have to be thawed.

Conclusion

Intermittent fasting has been used throughout history as a way of life. However, in the modern era, we have forgotten this aspect of life, and because of it, our health is suffering. Intermittent fasting has been shown to improve cholesterol, manage blood pressure, increase weight loss, reduce the risk of developing cancer, and much more. Thankfully, we can regain these benefits, as scientific studies have found that people who incorporate intermittent fasting into their daily lives become healthier and can better manage their weight.

You won't believe how easy it is to stick to intermittent fasting, because it is not a diet. You can still enjoy all your favorite foods in moderation. Although, it is best to pair intermittent fasting with a healthy diet and lifestyle for optimal results and health. But, this is nothing to worry about. It is much easier to eat healthy foods than you might think, and we have provided you with a number of such recipes that you can enjoy on a daily basis.

Intermittent fasting can fit perfectly into your life, allowing you to still enjoy meals with family and going out with friends. Not only that, but it is becoming more popular than ever, meaning that you can easily discuss your new lifestyle with your friends if you desire.

What are you waiting for? Health and weight loss are a few steps away, you only have to take the first step. I assure you, once you begin your journey of intermittent fasting you will never want to go back.

Intermittent Fasting for Women Over 50

The Winning Formula to Lose Weight, Unlock Your Metabolism and Rejuvenate Above 50's

[13 Anti-Aging Tips Included]

By

Austin Harris

Table of Contents

Disclaimer

This book is not a substitute for medical advice. All information and tools presented within this text are intended for motivational purposes.

Any health, diet or exercise advice shared here is not intended as medical diagnosis or treatment. If you think you have any type of medical condition you must seek professional advice even if you believe it may be due to diet, food or exercise. You should always consult a qualified practitioner before using any dietary, exercise or health advice from this text.

INTRODUCTION

THE BENEFITS OF FASTING

Fasting is not something that most of us ever think about – food is everywhere and, in all likelihood, right now you're within striking distance of an emergency skinny latte and a muffin. Now I love food as much as the next person, so what I find great about fasting is that it's as much about eating delicious things as it is about abstaining. And there are none of the harmful effects you get from following crazy diets or popping pills, because fasting provides a natural high, an inner boost that works with your body, not against it.

When I first learned about fasting, it was in the context of an invitation to join an intensive meditation retreat in the Himalayas. In fact, I only stumbled across meditation in a foggy, end-of-yoga-class kind of way (and usually ended up snoring!). By contrast, I'd always been fascinated by the inner poise of people who did yoga. I didn't just envy their lithe bodies – I wanted their unshakable contentment and smiling eyes. How did they manage to waft around so effortlessly and have boundless energy for eye-watering yoga moves? And they all seemed to look incredibly youthful and naturally glowing. What was their secret? Whatever it was, I had to have it. So, as you do when you are childless and too young to care about a job and responsibilities, I gave up a regular salary and sold my worldly possessions to enjoy an alternative (and rather late) gap year in an Indian ashram where I planned to study yoga and meditation. Admittedly, it was the thought of becoming supple and slender rather than discovering nirvana that sweetened the deal for me. As it happened, one of the simplest techniques I learned over those intensive months has become one of my most important life lessons for mind and body – how to fast.

Fasting is so easy; you really can't fail. In fact, it's something we all do already – breakfast, quite literally, is breaking a fast of around 12 hours. And let's not forget one of the best things of all – if you "do" fast properly (there are several techniques to choose from and by the end of the book you will discover which one suits you), you can finally give up on the endless hamster wheel of weight loss and gain that sees otherwise sane and successful people becoming slaves to whatever dieting fad happens to be the flavor of the month. I know the pain of that world because I existed in it for so long. I also know how good it feels to be free of it.

FASTING VERSUS OTHER WEIGHT-LOSS APPROACHES

It's time to stick my neck out. I'd go as far to say that I see fasting as the future of weight loss. The diet industry is just that – an industry – and a great many consumers have woken up to the fact that they have been sold a dummy. As any seasoned dieter knows, behind the hype and celebrity following, many trendy diet plans are just plain silly and impractical.

Long-term calorie restriction, the backbone of traditional weight loss, can make you prone to weight gain. Not only that, the nutritional aspects of many commercially savvy weight-loss plans are at best borderline, and at worst downright dangerous. The fact that one of the largest dieting companies in the world is owned by a confectionery company illustrates (to me at least) that the industry behind dieting and the promise of weight loss may need a bit of a shake-up.

Fundamentally, fasting for weight loss is all about nutrition. When you do eat, you must eat well. When you're fasting, there's no cutting out of major food groups such as carbohydrates or essential fats. In this book you'll find lots of information about what to eat when you adopt a fasting regime, rather than simply calculating when you don't eat. In fact, nutrition is even more important when you're fasting since you're eating less overall.

If I'm right and fasting becomes the next big thing in dieting, what will happen? Well, fasting is already rapidly gaining in popularity and when a trend begins – particularly a global trend – newspaper headlines don't necessarily get all the facts right. And when a trend imbibes the collective consciousness, particularly in weight loss, you can guarantee that money-wasting gimmicks will follow. Therefore, as part of your induction into the world of fasting, I'll be giving you a gimmick-free tour of the scientifically backed benefits of fasting for weight loss, longevity and performance.

Every piece of advice in this book is sound and practical. In my research I've discovered that in order to achieve the best results, fasting techniques should be subtly different for women and men, and different again if you're using fasting to enhance performance. Whilst science acts as the perfect signpost, we're all unique – biologically, physically and emotionally, and ultimately it remains your job and your job alone to turn evidence into action.

Even with the greatest advances, there are certain things that science, or nutrition for that matter, can't explain fully but I will nevertheless attempt to describe how fasting may make you feel more connected and happier in yourself. Fasting, more than any other nutrition or diet approach, can help you to reset your attitude and recognize the difference between physical hunger and appetite. Slowing down your eating can make the experience as much a "mental break" as a physical boost. Indeed, fasting has been used for centuries as a method of mental and spiritual purification. It's like setting a part of you free again.

THE SCIENCE ON FASTING

The scientific studies on fasting focus largely on alternate-day fasting and on prolonged periods of fasting. Much of the scientific research is done on animals rather than on humans – mainly because it's considered unethical to starve people for no reason! However, the evidence that is out there about the benefits of fasting is just so compelling and exciting that it's worthy of a few minutes of your attention (and I'll be busting several dieting myths along the way).

The following are a few highlights from the science of fasting that we'll explore in the forthcoming chapters:

FASTING FOR WEIGHT LOSS

- It might seem counter-intuitive, but intermittent fasting could help you get your hunger under control. This is partly because of its effects on your hunger hormones, and partly because it helps you to learn the difference between physical and emotional hunger.
- Forget what you've been told about regular meals boosting metabolism – studies show that people who are overweight tend to snack more often.
- Fasting is just as effective as traditional diets for losing weight, but might be easier to stick to and less likely to slow your metabolism – perfect if you want to lose that last bit of stubborn flesh.
- If you're stressed, and troubled by weight around your middle, shorter fasts may be better at tackling belly fat than longer ones.

FASTING FOR HEALTH

- Fasting – especially in combination with eating less protein – acts like a "spring clean" for the body by switching on a cellular mechanism called autophagy and by reducing the levels of a hormone called insulin-like growth factor (IGF-1) that can send cell growth out of control.

- Regular juice fasts may deliver potent anti-ageing benefits without you having to cut out food completely.

- Whichever fasting format you choose, it's likely to reduce inflammation – good news for conditions such as eczema, asthma and arthritis.

- Contrary to the popular belief that sugary snacks are "brain food", fasting may help adults to concentrate better. It could even help to build new brain cells.

FASTING FOR WOMEN

- The effects on blood sugar control seem to be different in women and men. Studies suggest that fasting improves men's blood sugar control, but may not have a beneficial effect on women.

- Most women know that adopting any new healthy habit is generally more challenging the week before their period starts. So, my advice is to go easy that week. Your nearest and dearest will be thankful too.

- When it comes to the overall impact of fasting on menstrual cycles, we only have animal studies to go on, and the effects aren't clear. However, any improvements in overall diet usually go some way to helping with any menstrual problems – so make sure you pay as much attention to what you do eat as you do to what you don't eat. If you notice any negative changes, or have lost weight to the point where your periods become disrupted, stop fasting.

FASTING FOR GYM BUNNIES

- Doing weight training while fasting can help your body build more muscle.

- If you favor cardio workouts, training while fasting can help your body learn to tap into its fat stores more intensively – but it's not such a good idea to run a race without eating beforehand.

- Again, there are gender differences – men tend to build muscle so long as they work out before their main meal, whereas women seem to respond better to training after a meal.

Part 1

Knowledge (The Winning Formula to Lose Weight)

Chapter One

EAT, FAST AND LOSE WEIGHT

Fasting simply means extending the time between meals when we don't eat, and is something that humans have practiced since they first walked the planet. It's only in recent times that we've had access to food 24 hours a day. Before then, we typically went for extended periods without eating. Fasting's no passing "fad" – unlike the modern trend of "grazing", the notion that we should constantly be ingesting small amounts. Interest in when and what we eat and drink has been increasing steadily and is set to continue. Nutritional knowledge helps us understand how our bodies and minds work, and nutritional intervention has a major role to play in the lives of everyone, from Olympic athletes to busy mums and people with medical conditions. No longer seen as something "alternative", nutritional therapy has now gone mainstream.

FASTING TODAY

Celebrities are usually the first to focus attention on any technique that involves the body beautiful, and fasting is no exception. So, as part of my research for this book, I went in search of some of the world's most famous celebrity personal trainers to ask them if they use fasting with their clients.

I've used intermittent fasting on many occasions – notably when people need to lose those last 2–4.5kg [5–10lb], or in order to stimulate stubborn fat loss. I have one client who fasts every Wednesday, just drinks water, green tea, some amino acids, and that's it, and that works very well for her. There are many protocols for fasting and each individual can use the one that works best for them. As with all diets though, the protocol needs to be sustainable so it can be implemented into a lifestyle."

If you still believe that fasting is just another passing diet fad – here today, gone tomorrow – think again. As I mentioned in the Introduction, I predict that fasting will not only become the next big global health trend but that it's here to stay. From a professional point of view, a technique that gets results without compromising health, that helps restore a sense of calm in the mind, and that costs nothing to do, kind of has it all.

THE TRUTH ABOUT FAT AND WEIGHT LOSS

These days, in countries where there's an abundance of food, we've become used to constant grazing – rarely sitting down for meals and simply picking at high-calorie, high-fat and high-sugar foods all day long. We've forgotten what it feels like to be really physically hungry.

The unfortunate truth is that many of us are designed to get fat. It all comes down to evolution. Back in the dim and distant past, when food shortages were common, people who had substantial fat "in storage" were more likely to survive.

Research carried out in the last century proved that extended periods of starvation are much less dangerous for people who have high levels of body fat – in fact, the heavier you are, the more likely it is that fasting will lead to substantial fat loss with muscle being spared. In contrast, the slimmer you are (and your ancestors were), the more likely it is that you'll break down muscle through extreme dieting.

People often blame their genes for a "slow metabolism" or "big bones", but it turns out things are more complicated than that. The genetic factors that helped your ancestors lay down fat stores seem to relate to a complex range of factors rather than simply affecting your metabolic rate. For example, there are subtle differences in appetite, or in the tendency to fidget.

WHY SOME PEOPLE ARE NATURALLY SLIM

Emerging research suggests that naturally slim people have genetic advantages that make it easier for them to avoid weight gain. They're not blessed with faster metabolisms, but tend to be able to regulate their appetite and burn off excess calories without even noticing it.

TO THEM, FOOD IS JUST FOOD

Naturally slim people enjoy food, but they don't have a strong emotional connection to it. Foods aren't "good" or "bad", they're just food. Therefore, slim types don't feel guilty when they tuck into a slice of cake or have a few chips with their dinner.

THEY CAN STOP AFTER JUST ONE BITE

When our naturally slim friends eat indulgent foods, they can stop after just a little, rather than polishing off the plate. Many of us are familiar with that feeling of having broken the diet rules:

"That's today ruined… I may as well finish the whole cake and start again tomorrow."

Slim people don't get that "all-or-nothing" feeling that's typical in seasoned dieters.

THEY RECOGNIZE THE DIFFERENCE BETWEEN HUNGER AND APPETITE

The mechanisms controlling our appetites are complex. Research suggests that naturally slim people may be more resistant to appetite signals that aren't linked to physiological hunger. What this means is, they eat when their body needs nourishment, not when their brain is trying to trick them into believing they're hungry. In contrast, those of us with a genetic tendency to gain weight can feel physically hungry when tempted by food, even if our bodies don't need the calories.

THEY BURN IT OFF

There's a theory that our body weight has a "set point" (a natural weight at which it tries to maintain itself). When a naturally slim person overeats, they tend to compensate by moving around more, without even thinking about it. So, as well as a few more gym sessions, they may fidget, get stuck into cleaning the house, or walk rather than taking the car. But for the majority of us, overeating is followed by a few hours relaxing on the sofa!

OTHER FACTORS INFLUENCING WEIGHT

Ultimately, weight gain comes down to the fact that we're eating more calories than we're burning off, and over time this has led to many of us gradually getting fatter. But tackling the issue is about more than simply cutting calories. The quality of what we eat is important too. The types of food that are so readily available to us – those muffins and sugary drinks – tend to be packed with sugar or refined carbohydrates (carbs) and it's very easy to eat them and not notice when we're full. Instead, try replacing those "empty" calories with nutrient-rich, lean proteins, leafy green vegetables and even healthy fats from nuts and oily fish. I promise you; these will make you feel full and you'll be much less tempted to overeat.

It's also important to detect underlying problems or habits that can be causing or contributing to a weight problem. For example, stress, emotional eating or chemical calories may have been the tipping point for your body. Unhealthy eating can mean that you're not getting enough of the vitamins, minerals and essential fats that your body needs to function well. What's more, many "fad" diets aren't nutritionally balanced, so they starve the body of the vital nutrients your body needs.

On a basic level, these problems can make it very hard for you to stick to a diet. Likewise, "crash" diets tend to drastically restrict your body's intake of calories. If your body isn't getting the nutrients it needs, the result can be irritability, depression and even lowered brain function, all of which inevitably affect your motivation to continue with the diet. And when you come off the diet, you quickly return to your previous weight and may end up gaining even more weight. This is because, when you lose weight, your metabolic rate naturally dips – more about this shortly.

STRESS AND WEIGHT GAIN

The link between stress and weight gain begins with tiny glands called adrenals. Their basic task is to rush all your body's resources into "fight or flight" mode by increasing production of adrenaline and other hormones – you may recognize this feeling with an increased heart rate, and your blood pressure may be raised.

Unlike our ancestors, who weren't distracted by mobile phones, deadlines, emails and the multi-tasking challenges of modern life, today we live under constant stress. Instead of occasional, acute demands followed by rest, we're constantly over-worked, under-nourished, exposed to environmental toxins, and plagued by worries… with no let-up.

Every challenge to the mind and body creates a demand on the adrenal glands. The result is a state of constant high alert and high levels of the hormone cortisol in the body, leading to a huge number of health problems, such as a tendency to hold on to stubborn belly fat. The other main side- effects of stress and adrenal overload are digestive problems, rapid ageing, lowered immunity and skin problems.

Sometimes it's less about the stress in our lives and more about the stress we place on ourselves with what we eat and drink. Take caffeine, for example. We're all familiar with the "buzz" that caffeine can give. Many products are marketed solely on the basis of this false energy kick, but that lively feeling is actually the sensation of adrenaline being pumped around the body as a result of the caffeine hit. The adrenal glands tire of constant stimulation and when the inevitable adrenal fatigue kicks in, it leads to a slowdown in the conversion of stored fats (and proteins and carbohydrates) into energy. We experience this failure in the energy chain as a craving for further stimulants in the form of more caffeine from another cup of tea, coffee, cola drink or caffeinated beverage. The last piece of the picture with caffeine is what usually comes with it. Remember that an average coffee these days contains a sizeable portion of milk, sugar or syrup and then there's the ubiquitous temptation of a muffin or pastry accompaniment!

INSULIN RESISTANCE AND THE EFFECTS OF ALCOHOL

When the body is overloaded with carbs (which are extremely commonplace in the average Western diet), it has to respond by making more insulin. Carbs are broken down into molecules of the sugar glucose, and insulin is the hormonal "key" that unlocks the cells to allow the glucose in. Over a period of time, excess insulin affects the cells by making them less sensitive to taking sugars into the cell and creating energy. This in turn prevents the cells from burning fat. The good news is that fasting may improve how your body handles sugar and help your body burn fat instead of storing it.

As far as your body's concerned, alcohol is chemically similar to sugar, so drinking any form of alcohol will set off the same insulin resistance seesaw that can promote weight gain. And that's before you even begin to consider the calorie content of the drink itself, which is likely to be very high and devoid of any nutritional benefit – so-called "empty calories". What's more, alcohol acts as a potent appetite booster, so more alcohol equals more food consumed!

There's yet another reason behind alcohol's "beer belly" effect. Alcohol reduces the amount of fat your body burns for energy, while preventing the absorption of many of the essential nutrients needed for successful weight loss, particularly the B vitamins and vitamin C. In one study published in the American Journal of Clinical Nutrition, eight men were given two glasses of vodka with diet lemonade, each containing just under 90 calories. For several hours after drinking the vodka, the amount of fat the men burned dropped by a massive 73 percent. Because your body uses more than one source of fuel, if alcohol is consumed then this alcohol "energy" will be used instead of fat – not good news for the waistline!

EMOTIONAL EATING

As we all know, a lot of eating is emotionally driven. Many people with weight problems fear feeling hungry. Furthermore, reaching for the sugar-fix from food or from alcohol is what helps free us, temporarily, from whatever uncomfortable emotion we might be feeling. Of course, sometimes an eating problem masks an underlying psychological problem or challenge. In such cases, expert advice, counselling or psychotherapy or psychology can really help.

Even when eating is free from emotional factors, the fact is, the longer you spend on a diet (whether for health or for weight loss), the less strict you become and the more likely it is that calories will sneak in without you noticing – a bite of this here, a nibble of that there. Fasting shakes up this model of eating altogether. Having a large section of the day when food simply isn't allowed to pass your lips prevents random snacking, and might also alert you to how often you do this normally. If you'd describe yourself as someone with limited self- control, fasting is an easier option than almost any other diet out there as you don't have to count every calorie or become a slave to food group fads – the only thing you really need to do is watch the clock.

"CHEMICAL CALORIES"

It's thought that chemicals in the environment have a blocking effect on the hormones that control weight loss. When the brain is affected by these toxins, hormone signaling can be impaired. Reducing chemicals in our homes, foods and drinks is important when looking at the overall picture of weight loss and health. As you'll discover in the "Nutritional Rules for Fasting" chapter, one of my nutrition rules as part of any fasting program me is to eat real food rather than fake food. If you can't pronounce what it says on the label, you probably shouldn't be eating it!

THYROID PROBLEMS

An underactive thyroid can cause weight gain, too. Symptoms include fatigue, cold, hormonal problems, depression and low libido as well as unexplained weight gain. The challenge is sometimes that the problem is sub- clinical, in other words, your test from the doctor may come back negative but you still have the symptoms. This can be frustrating for the sufferer as it sometimes means a re-visit in six months to a year to see if the symptoms register as qualifying for medical intervention.

A nutritious diet designed with thyroid health in mind can help. For the thyroid to work optimally, it needs nutrients such as iodine, manganese, vitamin C, methionine, magnesium, selenium, zinc, and the amino acids cysteine and L-tyrosine. These are all found in healthy foods such as fruit, vegetables, nuts, seeds and meat.

WHY TRADITIONAL DIETING MAKES YOU HUNGRY

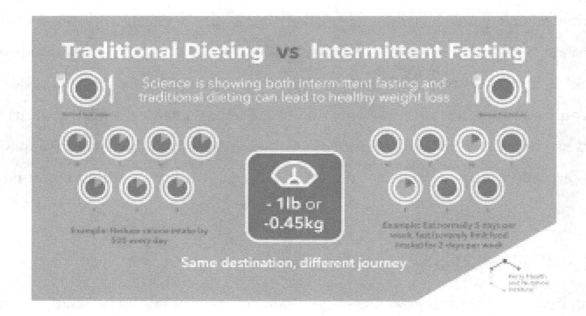

Going on a traditional diet without adequate energy intake for long periods of time can make your metabolic rate plummet and your appetite soar. Say you reduce your calories to below 1,000 a day for a number of weeks to fit into a party dress, the chances are you'll feel hungry and fed up much of the time, and as soon as the party starts, you'll dive head first into all the foods you've been avoiding, re-gaining that lost weight in no time! This, in a nutshell, sums up the seesaw of the diet industry.

The real trick is to keep your body feeling fuller for longer. I'm not talking about choosing one ready-meal over another, it's about understanding how to manage hunger so you naturally eat less most of the time. Please note, I don't say all of the time. Special events and over-indulging every now and then are good for the soul.

In tandem with a good diet overall, fasting can be used to retrain your hunger without the need for appetite suppressants or dodgy supplements. When you begin to fast, you will feel hungry at your usual meal times. However, if you choose not to eat at that time, the peaks and troughs of hunger start to level out. All this happens without a decrease in metabolic rate. It doesn't take a genius to recognize that if you feel hungry less often, you'll eat less and therefore lose weight. There's a biological explanation for this. Feelings of hunger and satiety (feeling full) are controlled by two main hormones produced within the body, ghrelin (even the word sounds hungry) and leptin. This dynamic duo of hormones has a powerful effect on how much food you eat and how much of what you've consumed you "burn off".

GHRELIN

This hormone seems pretty straightforward. When your stomach's empty, it sends out some ghrelin to tell an area of your brain, the hypothalamus, that you ought to be eating. You then feel ravenous. But research published in the American Journal of Physiology suggests that ghrelin levels also rise in anticipation of eating – you get hungry partly because you're expecting a meal, not just because you have an empty stomach.

On a traditional diet, you get a peak of ghrelin before every meal – but because you don't eat as much as you'd really like to, you never feel fully satisfied. When you're fasting, your ghrelin levels still rise, but anecdotal evidence suggests that over time your body finds this sensation easier to get used to, probably because of the changes in your meal patterns. There's also a theory that a nutritionally poor diet sends ghrelin rocketing faster than a nutrient-dense plan like the ones I recommend.

WHY MOST DIETS FAIL

This probably isn't the first book about weight loss you've ever read. I often say I've been down the diet road myself so many times that I could be a tour guide. If you're asking yourself why fasting is going to be any different, here are the facts you need to know:

•   "Yo-yo" dieting is the bane of many people's lives, but even if you've lost and gained weight countless times, recent research has shown that it's possible to lose weight safely without messing up your metabolism.

•   Burning off more calories than you eat is the only way to lose weight – and the simple truth is that you will lose weight if you manage to keep the number of calories you eat below the amount you burn off… boring but true.

There are hundreds of different ways to create a calorie deficit – as evidenced by the huge diet book, diet shake, diet bar and "miracle" weight-loss supplement industry. But there are two main reasons why diets never tend to live up to their expectations, especially as you get closer to your goal weight:

1   Traditional diet misrepresent the calories in/calories out equation.

We've all heard that 450g (1lb) of fat is roughly equal to 3,500 calories, so the traditional calorie-counting approach is to cut calories by 500–1,000 per day in order to lose 450–900g (1–2lb) per week. The trouble is, as you get slimmer you become lighter and that actually reduces the number of calories you burn at rest (your basal metabolic rate). So, in traditional weight-loss plans, weight loss is initially rapid but tends to slow down over time, even if you maintain that original calorie deficit. This can be very demotivating.

2   It's sticking to your chosen approach that's often the hard part.

Even if you get your calories exactly right, how boring does counting every calorie get? Demotivation – either as a result of not seeing the numbers on the scales going down as quickly as they were, or boredom – can lead to lapses, which slow down the rate of weight loss even further. When you go back to your old eating habits – surprise, surprise – you'll gain all the weight back, and a little more, as a result of the natural dip in basal metabolic rate (calorie burn) caused by your initial weight loss.

HOW FASTING MAKES A DIFFERENCE

FASTING MAY BOOST METABOLIC RATE

You're probably thinking, "If I start starving myself, won't that be worse for my metabolism?" First of all, fasting is not starving yourself, and don't worry that eating less often will damage your metabolism. Losing weight naturally slows your basal metabolic rate (the number of calories you burn at rest) in proportion to the amount of weight you lose, no matter which method you use. This is because your daily energy (calorie) needs are directly related to your age, height, gender and weight, in particular your lean body mass (muscle). It doesn't mean that eating more often will fire up your metabolism.

You'll hear over and over again that after a night of sleep, your metabolism has ground to a halt and you need to eat breakfast to stoke your metabolic fire. The idea that "breakfast boosts metabolism" is simply not true – it hasn't been backed up by research at all. The breakfast myth is based on the "thermic effect of food". Around 10 percent of our calorie burn comes from the energy that we use to digest, absorb and assimilate the nutrients in our meals. Roughly speaking, if you eat a 350-calorie breakfast, you'll burn 35 calories in the process. But notice that you've eaten 315 extra calories to burn that 35. No matter what time of day you eat, you'll burn off around 10 percent of the calories in your food through the thermic effect of food. So, whether you eat your breakfast at 7am, 10am or never, if you eat roughly the same amount and types of food overall, its effect on your metabolism will be the same.

In fact, all the research on fasting seems to show that eating less often could actually boost your metabolic rate. In one British study conducted at the University of Nottingham, a two-day fast boosted participants' resting metabolic rate by 3.6 percent. In another study by the same research group, 29 healthy men and women fasted for three days. After 12–36 hours, there was a significant increase in basal metabolic rate, which returned to normal after 72 hours. The exact mechanisms for why this happens aren't clear.

FASTING INCREASES FAT BURN

What is clear is that more of the calories you use for fuel during fasting come from your fat stores. Scientists can estimate what proportion of your energy is coming from fats and carbohydrates by measuring the amount of oxygen inhaled and the amount of carbon dioxide exhaled in your breath. The higher the proportion of oxygen to carbon dioxide, the more fat you're burning. As part of the same Nottingham study, findings proved that the proportion of energy obtained from fat rose progressively over 12–72 hours, until almost all the energy being used was coming from stored fat. This is incredible news really!

We're so often told to "breakfast like a king, lunch like a prince and dine like a pauper" with a view to becoming healthy, wealthy and wise. This is usually explained by telling us that breakfast kick-starts the metabolism – but it turns out that eating breakfast doesn't boost your fat-burning potential at all. In a small study on breakfast-eaters – published in the British Journal of Nutrition – a 700-calorie breakfast inhibited the use of fat for fuel throughout the day. Put simply, when we eat carbohydrates, we use it for fuel, and this prevents our bodies tapping into our stubborn stored fat. Constant grazing might be what's keeping fat locked away in your belly, bum or thighs – and fasting is one way to release it.

FASTING MAINTAINS LEAN MUSCLE

The more muscle you have, the more calories you burn at rest. And before you say you don't want big muscles, another way to put that is: the less muscle you lose as you drop in weight, the less your basal metabolic rate falls as you move toward your goal weight. (Remember, your basal metabolic rate is the rate at which you burn calories, so it's really important in order to make staying in shape easier in the long term.) Besides, muscle takes up less room than fat. So, a person with good lean muscle mass will take a smaller dress size or use a narrower belt notch than someone who doesn't have it.

Fasting is better than plain old calorie restriction when it comes to maintaining lean body mass. This is largely because fasting triggers the release of growth hormone (GH), which encourages your body to look for other fuel sources instead of attacking its muscle stores. This is thought to be a survival advantage – back when humans were hunter gatherers it wouldn't have made sense for our muscle mass to reduce when food was scarce – we needed strong legs and arms to hunt down our dinner!

In one study carried out by researchers at Intermountain Medical Center in the USA, participants were asked to fast for 24 hours. During this time, GH levels rose by a whopping 1,300 percent in women and 2,000 percent in men.

It's important to note that more isn't necessarily better when it comes to GH – what's key is resetting the balance between GH release (which happens in the fasted state) and insulin release (which happens in the fed state, however small your meal) in order to stimulate fat loss without losing lean muscle. You never need to fear growing giant muscles as a result of fasting – GH is released in waves and goes back to normal levels quickly as soon as your body has released enough fat to burn.

As mentioned earlier, if you're already slim, it's especially important not to overdo it when fasting. Research published in the academic journal Obesity Research shows that within just two days of complete fasting, there's a dramatic increase in the use of muscle for fuel in people who are already a healthy weight. This is because they have less fat available to burn overall. Perhaps the advice for people who are already svelte but who want to fast for health benefits is to fast little and often rather than to eat little and often.

FASTING PATTERNS GIVE YOU ENERGY WHEN YOU NEED IT

Alongside maintaining your muscle mass to reduce the dip in your metabolic rate that happens as you lose weight, fasting may help with stubborn weight in other ways.

There's a theory that the reduction in calorie burn typically seen after following a calorie-restricted diet may be related more to changes in activity level than to basal metabolic rate. When you're only eating, say, 1,200 calories day after day, it may be difficult to maintain the energy levels and motivation to exercise. But following an intermittent fasting pattern means that you can concentrate your workouts around the times when you're eating. More energy means a tougher workout – and more calorie burn overall.

COMMON QUESTIONS AND ANSWERS

Q   Isn't "not eating" dangerous?

A   It's very important to establish that fasting is not starvation, which, of course, is dangerous. What I'm talking about is the health benefits of increasing the gaps between meals or eating less from time to time.

Some people who are fully signed up to the merry-go-round of traditional dieting will argue that not eating is likely to induce a low-blood-sugar or "hypo" episode. Feeling faint, clammy and unable to concentrate are typical symptoms, happily offset by a visit to the vending machine or, for the health- aware, a snack such as an oatcake or nuts and seeds. I'm not suggesting that snacking should be outlawed – most of the time, I'm more than happy to tuck right in. But fasting challenges the assertion that we can't survive, or even thrive, without five mini-meals a day.

Q   Won't I feel light-headed and really hungry on a fast?

A   You might be worried that your blood sugar levels will dip too low between meals and that you'll feel faint and weak. But when you're not eating, other hormonal signals trigger your body to release glucose or make more. In one Swedish study by researchers at the Karolinska Institute, students who'd reported that they were sensitive to hypoglycemia (low blood sugar) felt irritable and shaky during a 24-hour fast, but there was actually no difference in their blood sugar levels – it may all have been in their minds.

Q   Hang on a minute… My trainer told me that six small meals will fire up my metabolism and stop me feeling peckish. Who's right?

A   This is one of those fitness and nutrition "truths" that has been repeated so many times, people are convinced that it's a fact. In one small study at the US National Institute on Aging, researchers found that people who ate only one meal a day did tend to feel hungrier than those who ate three. But beyond eating three meals a day, meal frequency doesn't seem to make a difference to hunger or appetite, so it comes down to what's actually easiest for you. A study published by the International Journal of Obesity showed that people who are overweight tend to snack more often.

The truth is, you will feel hungry when fasting – there's no getting away from that – but rather than a constant unsatisfied feeling, your hunger will come in waves. You'll start to recognize the difference between physical and psychological hunger. And you'll get to eat meals that are big enough to leave you feeling genuinely satisfied when you do eat.

Q   Can fasting change my shape?

A   For many women, that last bit of surplus weight is carried around the hips and thighs and it simply won't shift. To solve this problem, I suggest looking to the true body professionals.

According to noted intermittent-fasting expert Martin Berkhan, there's a good reason for this. All the cells in our body have "holes" in them known as receptors. To switch activity on and off in those cells, hormones or enzymes enter the receptors. Fat cells contain two types of receptor – beta 2 receptors, which are good at triggering fat burning, and alpha 2 receptors, which aren't. Guess which is mostly found in the fat stores of your lower body? Yes, our hips and thighs have nine times more alpha 2 receptors than beta.

Fasting is the only thing that alters alpha 2 receptor expression in adults – when we're fasting, the alpha 2 receptors are more likely to stay hidden. If you combine this with the fact that GH and catecholamines (hormones released by the adrenal glands) are particularly good at encouraging fat loss, then fasting is a way for your body to release the stubborn fat it retained while you were on traditional diets.

Q   What about belly fat?

A   All over the Internet you'll see promises that you can get rid of belly fat in a matter of days by taking supplements. We all know that this is simply not true.

Stubborn fat around the middle is linked to a number of factors – including stress, alcohol, lack of exercise and a diet high in refined carbohydrates.

Stress + refined carbohydrates + alcohol = a recipe for belly fat, especially if you're unlucky enough to be genetically predisposed to weight gain around the middle.

Q   How does fasting help torch belly fat?

A   To burn belly fat, free fatty acids must first be released from your fat cells (this is called lipolysis) and moved into your bloodstream, then transferred into the mitochondria of muscle or organ cells, to be burned (a process known as beta-oxidation).

Glucagon (another pancreatic hormone that has pretty much an equal and opposite effect to insulin) rises around four to five hours after eating, once all the digested nutrients from your last meal have been stored or used up. The purpose of glucagon is to maintain a steady supply of glucose to the brain and red blood cells, which it achieves by breaking down stored carbohydrates and leftover protein fragments in the liver. It also activates hormone-sensitive lipase, which triggers the release of fat from the fat cells, allowing other cells to be fueled by fat as opposed to glucose.

Q What else can I do to help get rid of belly fat?

A Endurance exercise selectively reduces abdominal fat and aids maintenance of lean body mass, so it's great to do in combination with intermittent fasting. Choose a fasting method that will enable you to take regular exercise – gentle activity such as walking will help, but high-intensity training is even better.

Also, a very small recent study, carried out at the University of Oklahoma in the USA, found that quality protein intake was inversely associated with belly fat, so make sure you fuel up on lean proteins (which your fasting plans are rich in), when you are eating.

Q What about losing that last 4.5kg (10lb)?

A This is often the hardest weight to shift. Not only that, it tends to creep back over a matter of weeks after you've finally reached your target weight. A familiar story is the strict diet we follow to get into beach-body shape in time for a holiday: in all the years I've helped people to lose weight, I've lost count of the number of times I've heard people telling me that all their hard work was undone by two weeks of sun, sea and sangria!

Remember that losing weight is all about creating a calorie deficit. Here, fasting is acting in two different ways. First, fasting helps maintain calorie burn – so in theory you can eat more overall and still lose weight. Second, fasting might just be easier to stick to than a boring calorie-counting diet. And when it comes to beach bodies, remember that old saying "a change is as good as a rest". If you're bored of the approach you've taken to weight loss up to now, a short blast of fasting can help you achieve your goal weight without damaging your metabolism.

This is backed up by research. Most of the studies on intermittent fasting show that it can be just as effective for fat loss as traditional diets, but the studies are all designed differently so it's difficult to say exactly which fasting approach will be the most effective for you. Scientific studies on intermittent fasting have shown varying results – from an average weight loss of a few kilos in the first few days, to 8 percent of body weight within eight weeks.

During the first few days of the fast you'll generally lose weight quickly, which can feel very motivating, especially if the scales have been stuck for a while.

One thing to note is that your weight will fluctuate. At first, you'll lose water (because stored glucose holds roughly four times its weight in water, and is quickly used up during a fast), and yesterday's food should make its way through your digestive tract. Alongside this, you'll lose some body fat. But the next day, you'll gain weight via the new intake of water and food. Don't worry! Over time, your average weight will fall. That's why it's important to limit weighing yourself to once or twice a week, and to be consistent in the time and day you use the scales.

Part 2

Practice (Unlock Your Metabolism)

EAT, FAST AND LIVE LONGER

THE HEALING POWER OF FASTING

Over the last decade I've seen my clients achieve amazing results with fasting. Getting to the optimum weight for your body frame is as much about health as it is about looking and feeling good. Fasting improves health alongside helping to shift the pounds and, just as importantly, it can help heal somebody's relationship with food, which is often at the heart of the struggle with weight.

I firmly believe that what I can achieve with a client during a week of fasting would take me months or possibly years with a conventional nutrition approach. In fact, I'll stick my neck out and say that fasting can and will change how we as a society view healing – if someone told you there was a pill that could reduce the risk of diabetes, cancer and heart disease and keep you looking and feeling young, you'd be tempted to take it, wouldn't you?

Unlike medication, so long as you're sensible about it, there are no harmful side-effects of fasting. Contrast this with the side-effects of common prescription and over-the-counter drugs – even if the chance of side-effects is small, the risks are still real. One study published by the peer-reviewed British Medical Journal into the side-effects of statins (cholesterol-lowering drugs), confirmed cases of increased risk of muscle weakness, cataracts, acute kidney failure, and moderate or severe liver dysfunction. Of course, if disease has taken hold, the benefits of medication will often outweigh the risks. However, we need to be working toward a model of preventative action.

HOW FASTING PROMOTES HEALING

Nothing in the body, or mind, works in isolation, so it shouldn't come as a surprise to learn that fasting creates a healthy "ripple effect" of sorts.

The over-arching theory is that fasting helps to de-stress the body. When you fast, you give your body a break and a chance to catch up on its inner "to-do" list. We all know how good it feels to have a well-earned holiday and return rested, rejuvenated and with renewed joie de vivre. Well, fasting has a similar effect on your body.

Around 70 percent of your daily energy is spent maintaining internal functions, such as digestion and detoxification. If you're a busy, on-the-go person and don't give your body the best conditions to rest, digest and ultimately heal, ill-health will catch up with you sooner or later.

Have you ever had that sluggish feeling, much like a slow hangover that's really difficult to shake off? Just as your home or office can become dusty and dirty, so your body can become clogged up with toxins and waste matter from the environment around you (more about this later in the chapter). When your body is clean and strong, it's able to eliminate toxins efficiently, but when it becomes overloaded it can become sluggish, overweight (or underweight in some instances) and more susceptible to disease. The result is that "toxic signals", such as aches and pains, irritable bowel, skin complaints, mood swings and fatigue, start to kick in. If these signals are ignored, they allow longer-term chronic health problems to take hold.

Cue fasting. Thousands of studies or observations of both man and animals have established the fact that when the body goes without food, the tissues are called upon in an inverse order of their importance to the organism. What this means is that when you fast, fat is the first tissue to go. And, contrary to expectations, instead of food deprivation causing a debilitating loss of nutrients, in short-term fasts the body retains the majority of these.

Fasting is now considered an acceptable treatment or approach for promoting longevity, improving insulin response, reducing inflammation, boosting cardiovascular health and even for supporting cancer treatment. Fasting may deliver health benefits and more, without many of the unpleasant side-effects produced by other treatments, and, again, without an extortionate price tag.

FASTING AND ANTI-AGEING

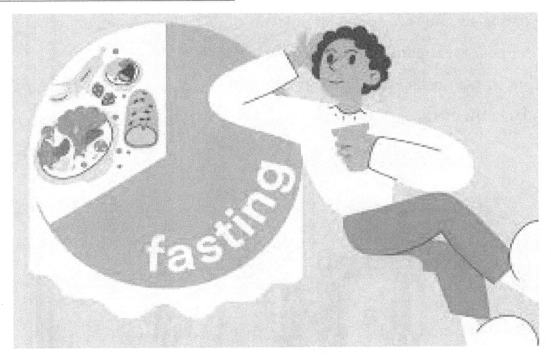

Ageing is inevitable. Everything that keeps us alive from one day to the next can be called your metabolism, and running your body has side-effects. Those side- effects accumulate and eventually will cause problems. Welcome to the reality of ageing… But reality is ever changing and there's good reason to be optimistic. Like looking for the proverbial pot of gold, we seekers of health are all out there, trying to find the elixir of youth.

You're as young or as old as your smallest vital links – your cells. Ageing begins when your normal process of cell regeneration and rebuilding slows down. At a cellular level, the hormone insulin-like growth factor (IGF-1) has both positive and negative effects. Like insulin, it's anabolic, meaning that, in effect, it tells our cells to grow and multiply. If IGF-1 is kept high, our cells constantly divide and multiply, which is good if we're trying to build big muscles and not so good if those cells become damaged and cancerous. High levels of IGF-1 have been linked to prostate cancer and post-menopausal breast cancer. When IGF-1 levels drop, the body slows production of new cells and starts repairing old ones, and DNA damage is more likely to be permanent.

KEEPING THE HEART AND CIRCULATION HEALTHY

Inflammation is involved in cardiovascular disease, in concert with high levels of "bad" fats in the blood. Most studies on fasting show that it reduces triglyceride levels and improves the ratio of triglycerides to "good" cholesterol (that is, high-density lipoprotein [HDL] – the transport protein that helps remove excess cholesterol from the bloodstream). In animal studies, resistance to what is known as "ischemic injury" – the type of artery damage that's associated with the build-up of plaques and hardening of the arteries – has been seen.

All in all, although the findings are far from clear and lots more research is needed, fasting seems to give the body an internal tune-up and to increase resistance to age-related illnesses.

Going back to those scary statistics from the beginning of this chapter – cardiovascular disease is the leading cause of death worldwide and something that affects us all. In Britain, NHS statistics show that in England in 2007, people aged over 60 were prescribed an average of 42.4 prescription items each. Each time you receive a prescription for an individual drug from your doctor, it counts as one prescription item. That's a whole lot of drugs! Unsurprisingly, medication that treats cardiovascular disease and its risk factors is the most commonly prescribed. I often meet people who want to change their eating habits, not just because they'd like to look and feel better, but because they're shocked by the amount of medication that their own parents are on. As fasting becomes more popular, people are becoming attracted to it as a lifestyle choice that might help their heart and circulatory system stay healthy for longer.

FASTING AND CANCER

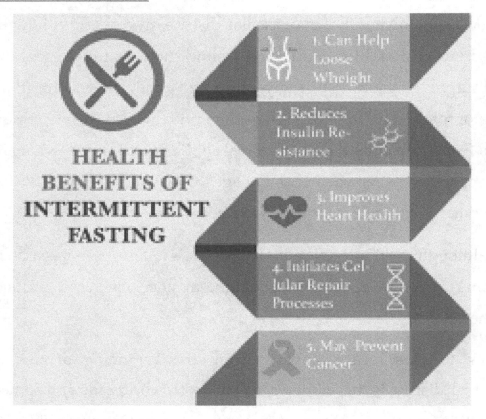

Fasting is considered to be an alternative or complementary treatment for cancer in certain sectors of complementary medicine, and has been popularized by a naturopathic doctor called Max Gerson. However, my focus is not on fasting as a stand-alone treatment but rather on exciting evidence about fasting in cancer prevention and the encouraging results from trials involving fasting during cancer treatment, particularly chemotherapy.

There's evidence that intermittent fasting, and calorie restriction more generally, fights the growth and spread of cancer cells in animals. Often when we read about research on animals, it seems so compelling that we want to see if the same thing will work for us. However, research is so much less likely to be done on humans as, rightly or wrongly, ethics committees are often reluctant to approve the same types of study that are done on animals. As discussed above, in experiments on laboratory animals, diets with 25 percent fewer calories have shown a positive link with longer, healthier life spans. So far there's little empirical study evidence to show the same effect in humans, yet anecdotal evidence is growing that restricting calories, and fasting, activates cell-protecting mechanisms. Research is also underway to find out whether alternate-day fasting can help reduce the risk of breast cancer.

In studies on mice with cancer, fasting appears to improve survival rates after chemotherapy. Hearing of the effects of these animal studies by Valter Longo, ten cancer patients took it upon themselves to try fasting before chemotherapy. The results were published in the medical journal Aging. Of these ten, the majority experienced fewer side-effects as a result of fasting than those eating normally, and the authors concluded that fasting for two to five days before chemotherapy treatment appeared to be safe. This work has yet to be taken to a truly meaningful empirical testing on humans, but it's understandable that cancer patients are excited by the potential of calorie restriction and fasting, not least by it helping the body to mitigate the effects of cancer treatment and specifically chemotherapy.

DETOXING

Personally, I no longer like the word "detox". It's been used and abused by marketeers in their quest to sell, sell, sell fancy products, when, in fact, detoxing is something that the body does naturally every hour of the day. However, until someone comes up with a better word, "detox" will have to do.

HOW WE BECOME TOXIC

A toxin is anything that has a detrimental effect on cell function or structure. Toxins are materials that our bodies cannot process efficiently. Over time they build up and, as a result, our systems function below par, leaving us drained, tired and frequently ill. People become "toxic" in many ways – through diet, lifestyle and the environment, as a natural by-product of metabolism, and through genetic lineage. Stress and harmful emotions can also create a kind of toxic environment.

Toxins include, but are not limited to:

- Food additives, flavorings and colorings.

- Household and personal cleaning chemicals, which are both inhaled and absorbed via the skin.

- Agricultural chemicals, such as pesticides, fungicides and herbicides.

- Heavy metals, which occur naturally but are poisonous.

• Oestrogens, which enter the environment due to human usage of the contraceptive pill and HRT.

• Xeno-oestrogens, which are chemicals that mimic oestrogen.

…And here are the most common ways people become toxic on the inside:

• Eating a poor diet. This includes low-fiber foods, fried foods and foods tainted with synthetic chemicals. Unlike live foods (fresh fruits and vegetables), these lack the enzymes that assist proper digestion and assimilation, and the fiber or bulk that assists proper elimination. They're also void of essential vitamins, minerals and other basic nutrients.

• Eating too much. Over-eating puts a great amount of stress on our digestive system. The body must produce hydrochloric acid, pancreatic enzymes, bile and other digestive factors to process a meal. When we over-eat, the digestive system finds it hard to meet the demands placed upon it. The stomach bloats as the digestive system goes into turmoil. Foods aren't broken down properly and tend to lodge in the lower intestine. Vital nutrients are then not absorbed.

• Inadequate water intake. When the body isn't receiving enough water, toxins tend to stagnate, hindering all digestive and eliminative processes.

• Exposure to synthetic chemicals in food and environmental pollutants. A clean, strong system can metabolize and excrete many pollutants, but when the body is weak or constipated, they're stored as unusable substances. As more and different chemicals enter the body, they tend to interact with those already there, forming second-generation chemicals that can be far more harmful than the originals.

• Being stressed. Stress hinders proper digestion, absorption and elimination of foods.

• Overuse of antibiotics. Antibiotics have a damaging effect on the intestines, especially if they're taken for extensive periods of time. Reducing the use of unnecessary antibiotics will also help minimize the very real danger of bacterial resistance.

• Lack of exercise. This lowers metabolic efficiency, and without circulatory stimulation, the body's natural cleansing systems are weakened.

• Eating late at night. The human body uses sleep to repair, rebuild and restore itself. In essence, the body uses the sleeping hours to cleanse and build. When a person goes to sleep with a full stomach, the body isn't at rest but is busy digesting and processing food. In addition, the body requires gravity to assist the passage of food from the stomach down the digestive tract.

Q   If the body detoxes itself anyway, why bother to do anything further?

A   Just as your home or office can become dusty and dirty, so your body can become clogged up with toxins and waste matter from the environment. A healthy body is able to disarm toxins by breaking them down, storing them in fat tissue or excreting them. However, here's the crux – many, if not most,

people are depleted in the nutrients needed to detox optimally, and chronic health problems, sluggishness and weight gain are common results.

If you've never given your digestion much thought, don't beat yourself up about being neglectful. Unlike the head or the tips of the fingers, the gut contains very few nerve endings. What this means is, we're not so aware when things aren't working well. When you have a headache, you feel every throbbing pulse and do something about it. In contrast, gut problems go unresolved and uncared for over long periods.

The good news is, when you improve digestion, a whole range of seemingly unrelated health issues can improve. For example, it's not only the job of the white blood cells (the leukocytes) to defend your body since the digestive system forms the basis of your immune system with the action of beneficial bacteria. Improving the ecology of the gut can be achieved with a juice fast and healthy diet.

USING A JUICE FAST TO DETOX

A juice fast stands head and shoulders above other fasting techniques in its self-healing effect and is often mentioned in the context of detoxing the body.

Juice fasting is based on consuming juices and broths only, whereas intermittent fasting adds lean protein and fat for the feeling of fullness. Studies have shown that eating as little as 10g (¼oz) of essential amino acids (found in high-quality proteins) can switch off autophagy. Therefore, a juice fast is best placed to give your body a good "spring clean" because juices are typically very low in protein.

The simple act of juicing a fruit or vegetable will help you absorb more of the nutrients from it. The caveat here is that you should make the juice fresh rather than drink pasteurized fruit juice from a carton or bottle. The process of juicing eliminates a lot of the fiber that needs to be digested. Cutting out the bulk and drinking only the juice means that you can very effectively hit your antioxidant targets in one small cup. Juice provides tiny "particles" of nutrients that are readily absorbed into the bloodstream.

Fresh juices provide a highly effective fast-track and – importantly – easy delivery mechanism for the body to absorb and process key vitamins, minerals and plant chemicals (phytonutrients) that are so beneficial to our health. A fresh juice contains a concentration of nutrients that have been separated from pulp, making it easier to consume what's required to assist the healing process. In essence, a fresh juice should be considered more of a body tonic than a tasty drink.

Q   Will I get withdrawal symptoms on a juice fast?

A   The folklore of fasting is littered with stories about the dramatic side-effects of a juice fast. This is usually because the contrast between the diet and lifestyle before and after is simply too great. Or, in some cases, the enterprising individual has decided to "retox", that is go on an almighty bender before entering detox – not a good idea.

One of the most dramatic side-effects I ever witnessed was when a client was coming off a 20-year-long diet cola habit during a juice-fasting retreat. Her symptoms were akin to what you'd expect from coming off a class-A drug. The rest of the detox group watched mesmerized at her descent from bubbly, bouncy guest on arrival to a sweating, vomiting, pale-faced shadow of her former self after just 24 hours of juicing. Even I was a little worried. Luckily, her troubled time was followed by a rapid and dramatic improvement two days later, at which point she declared that she felt "reborn" and would never touch a drop of cola again.

So, learn from my diet cola story and start with a transition diet. Fasting can be a challenge physically and psychologically. I recommend having at least three days on the Countdown Plan to prepare. Juice fasting should be undertaken for between one and five days for optimum results – usually once or twice a year. Any longer requires more management and should only be considered when there are adequate reserves (body fat) or if there's a specific medical condition. Some people find that weekend-long juice fasts four times a year are helpful.

Q   What are the most common side-effects of a juice fast?

A   Let me be frank – a juice fast isn't a good idea for a romantic break or naughty weekend away. During a juice fast the capacity of the eliminative organs – lungs, liver, kidneys, and skin – is greatly increased, and masses of accumulated metabolic wastes and toxins are quickly expelled. It's like pressing the accelerator button on your body's waste disposal unit. As part of the eliminative process, your body will be cleansing itself of old, accumulated wastes and toxins. This typically throws up symptoms such as offensive breath, dark urine, increased faecal waste, skin eruptions, perspiration and increased mucus. As I said, it's not exactly romantic!

Your digestive system is the star of a fasting program. Poor digestion can be a hidden cause of weight gain, or more accurately, water retention. For example, if your body's responding to an allergy or intolerance, it will often retain water. So, when fasting, there's often a "quick-win" water loss that equates to an extra kilo being lost.

Q   What about fiber?

A   The process of juicing extracts the pulp (fiber) of the fruits and vegetables so on a juice fast it's a good idea to restore some bulk to maintain a healthy transit of waste matter through the gastrointestinal tract. Psyllium husks, a soluble form of fiber, do just the trick as, when taken with adequate amounts of fluids, they absorb water to form a large mass. In people with constipation, this mass stimulates the bowel to move, whereas in people with diarrhea it can slow things down and reduce bowel movements.

Some recent research also shows that psyllium husks may lower cholesterol. It's thought that the fiber stimulates the conversion of cholesterol into bile acid and increases bile acid excretion. In addition, psyllium husks may even decrease the intestinal absorption of cholesterol.

Psyllium comes from the plant Plantago ovata and is native to India. It is readily available in health food shops and online stores, either as husks or in powdered form. In non-fasting, normal dietary conditions, whole grains provide dietary fiber and similar beneficial effects to psyllium, so a supplement isn't needed unless recommended by your health care practitioner.

Q   Can colon cleansing help?

A   Your bowels are not just "poo pipes". Toxins and metabolic wastes from the blood and tissues are discharged into the intestinal canal to be excreted from the body. Not surprisingly, one of the long-established techniques to support the body's elimination organs during a fast is colon hydrotherapy or enemas. This is a technique that involves taking in water into the large intestine, also known as the bowel, to assist the removal of waste.

Part 3

Results (Rejuvenate)

EAT, FAST AND PERFORM BETTER

CAN FASTING GIVE YOU A YOUNGER BRAIN?

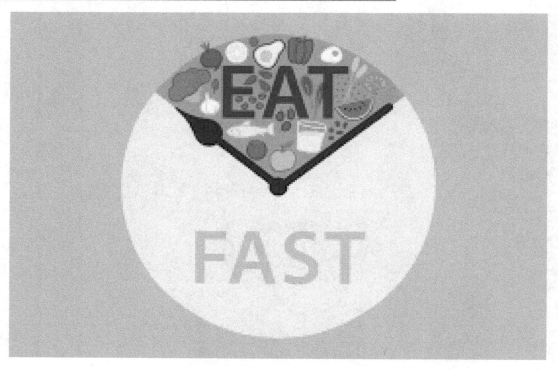

The potential benefits of fasting go beyond weight loss and physical health. If you've ever found yourself befuddled about where you could possibly have left your keys/phone/purse/marbles, you'll know that memory loss is a very frightening thing. The threat of long-term conditions like Alzheimer's is arguably one of the most worrying aspects of ageing. But there is hope. Researchers at the National Institute on Aging in Baltimore have found evidence that fasting for one or two days each week may help protect the brain against Alzheimer's, Parkinson's and other brain diseases.

ISN'T BREAKFAST IMPORTANT "BRAIN FOOD"?

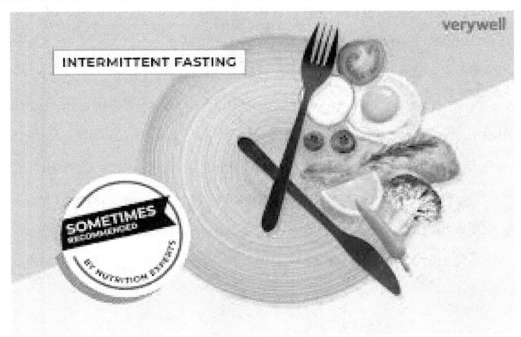

Children who eat breakfast tend to perform better in cognitive tests, but this doesn't seem to be the case for adults. Studies have shown that short-term food reduction doesn't actually impair cognitive function in adults. Prolonged dieting, on the other hand, does. This means that the perceived deterioration in brain function may, in fact, have a psychological cause – rather than being caused by a dip in blood sugar, lack of concentration may be a result of the stress of being "on a diet" (the way it tends to make you feel grumpy, miserable, and obsessive about food). Of course, it's true that the brain uses glucose for fuel, but as we've seen in previous chapters, our bodies have enough stored glucose to see us through a short fast.

In one study, published in the American Journal of Clinical Nutrition, scientists observed that fasting and non-fasting groups of adults performed similarly in cognitive tests, even after two days without food. This is thought to relate to adaptive mechanisms – as adults, when we don't have food available, it's important that we have the mental clarity to go out and find it. Our hunter- gatherer ancestors didn't have the option to pop out to the supermarket to grab a snack, and those who could think more clearly when hungry were more likely to be able to find food or outsmart predators. This was a survival advantage, and so the genetic factors that maintained cognitive function when food was scarce were passed on. As there haven't been dramatic changes in our genes since caveman times, it makes sense that the ability to think clearly when we haven't eaten for a while should still be the norm.

FASTING AND BRAIN HEALTH

Professor Mark Mattson, a renowned researcher at the National Institute on Aging, has dedicated his career to studying the effects of fasting on brain ageing. Until now, all his research has been on mice, but there's now enough evidence of the beneficial effects of fasting on the brains of mice to begin research on humans.

At the National Institute on Aging, mice have been bred to develop a susceptibility to Alzheimer's disease. If they are then put on a "fast food" diet which is high in sugar, they experience an earlier onset of learning and memory problems. But if they're made to fast every other day, they find it much easier to remember their way around a maze. Brain scans on the mice show that fasting actually encourages new brain cells (neurons) to form by placing a mild level of stress on the brain cells, which encourages them to build up a resistance to future stress, as well as building new proteins. Other researchers have found that fasting also increases the rate of autophagy in the brain, thereby getting rid of any damaged "grey matter" and making way for healthy new cells. So, while it's too early to tell whether fasting is the miracle cure for memory loss and age- related brain diseases, the research definitely sounds promising.

WHAT ELSE CAN I DO TO KEEP MY BRAIN YOUNG?

Sadly, the exact reasons why some people are susceptible to diseases such as Alzheimer's are unclear. It's generally accepted that diets rich in fruit, vegetables and healthy fats from fish, avocados and olives (typically like the Mediterranean diet) are associated with good brain health. What's good for the body is also good for the brain!

One of the most important things that you can do for your body and brain is to get active and regular fasting might just help you do that. Recent studies published in the Archives of Internal Medicine indicate that the more active we are as we get older – even if it's just gentle walking – the longer our brains will stay healthy. It sounds like the recipe for a healthy brain could be fasting combined with an active lifestyle and a real-food based diet – just what I have in mind!

CAN FASTING MAKE YOU FASTER?

I have to declare an interest here… For a few years I've loved the release that running has given me, especially after having my second baby. In fact, I've been a competitive soul from day dot. In my early youth I was good at badminton and represented Scotland in the game. In those days, not much attention was paid to sports nutrition, and since badminton is a largely anaerobic discipline it was possible to get by without thinking too much about what you were eating. Now, of course, everything has changed. Nutritionists feature large in all serious sport - not least, I imagine, because the "quick fix" route of banned substances has come under the spotlight, and, of course, we're all more aware of nutrition's role in exercise.

My running has become something of a "fix" – a means of releasing tension, either before the stress of the school run, or after the stress of a day's work. My usual preparation used to consist of an espresso and a mostly empty stomach. While that works for a quick half-hour run, it was only when I stepped up to training for the London Marathon in 2011 that I became more scientific and observant of my nutritional requirements. I also wondered whether fasting during training or pre-event could make a person run faster.

COMMON QUESTIONS AND ANSWERS

Q   What's the truth about sports drinks?

A   If you're a keen runner or cyclist, or harbor ambitions to run a marathon, you're probably aware of the importance of getting plenty of carbs. It's impossible to open up a running magazine or take part in a race without being bombarded with adverts for the latest energy drink or gel.

It's a fact that topping up your fuel levels with sugar – whether from fruit juice, sweets or expensive sports drinks – can make you run faster if your existing energy levels are low. Countless sports nutrition studies confirm that they do benefit performance. And the British public are buying into the dream en masse. In 2010, we drank 600 million liters of energy drinks and sports drinks.

However, topping up your blood sugar during exercise is only beneficial if you're taking part in high-intensity exercise that lasts for more than an hour, such as running a half-marathon or competing in a football match. In other cases, it won't do you any favors at all.

Q   What about fasting and exercise during Ramadan?

A   Interest in the effects of fasting on fitness has increased in recent years, inspired by studies on what happens to Muslim athletes during the month of Ramadan. During Ramadan, Muslims are required to observe a period of fasting from dawn until sunset. This includes avoiding not only food, but fluids too. As the dates of Ramadan change from year to year, this means that it can take place across major events in the sporting calendar, such as the 2012 Olympics. If you believe the sports nutrition adverts, you may think that not being able to eat or drink regularly would ruin an athlete's chances of winning, but that doesn't necessarily seem to be the case.

While most medal contenders at the 2012 Olympics seem to have taken the opportunity to postpone their fast until later in the year, in 1980 Tanzanian runner Suleiman Nyambui won silver in the 5,000 meters while observing the Ramadan fast. The effects of fasting on athletes' ability to compete and train during Ramadan are mixed. Several studies summarizing the research were published in the Journal of Sports Science in 2012. The overall picture was that the effects of fasting on performance are minimal, so long as overall nutritional intake and other factors, such as quality of sleep, are maintained.

Nevertheless, training while fasting – especially in the case of Ramadan, where athletes are also likely to be dehydrated through avoiding water – may make you feel more tired or reduce the amount of effort that you're able to put in. But, for mere mortals rather than Olympians, intermittent fasting has the promising ability to improve overall fitness or sports performance.

Q   Should I cut carbs?

A   As mentioned at the beginning of this chapter, the roots of how fasting may benefit performance are in our evolutionary past. Our caveman ancestors simply didn't have the opportunity to fuel up with carbohydrates before they went off to forage and hunt. Cycles of feast and famine meant that the ability to perform extended periods of physical activity on an empty stomach was an advantage when it came to survival. It's thought that our genetic make-up hasn't changed much in the 10,000 or so years since. So, it makes sense, in theory, that humans are designed to exercise without taking on extra fuel. At all times, our bodies burn both fat and carbohydrate for energy. While our storage capacity for carbohydrate is limited to around 500 calories-worth, most of us have more than enough fat stores to keep us going for a while. Say you're 70kg (11st) and your body fat is 25 percent – that means you have over 150,000 calories of fat in storage.

Aerobic training increases the proportion of fat to carbohydrate burned, making it easier to exercise for long periods of time. Just as the body adapts to any training stimulus by getting stronger or fitter, the idea is that training when fasting – when stored carbohydrate levels are low – stimulates the body to become even more efficient at using stored fat for fuel. While it might therefore seem like a no-brainer that exercising without extra carbohydrate will help your body adapt, it has long been recommended that endurance athletes consume a carbohydrate-rich diet.

Carbohydrate is stored in muscles as glycogen, where it can easily be broken down into glucose to fuel movement. Most research continues to emphasize the importance of adequate carbohydrate intake, before, during and after exercise. This is particularly important during high- intensity events, where glucose is the main fuel – stored fat is pretty good at fueling slow and steady movement, but it's glucose that your body turns to when you want to move fast. In events or training that last over an hour, it's generally recommended that 30–60g (1–2¼oz) of carbohydrate is consumed per hour, in the form of drinks, gels or food.

The mistake that many of us make is to rely on topping up our carbohydrate stores too much. This could also be the reason why many people don't lose weight when they start exercising. A typical bottle of sports drink can take half an hour of leisurely cycling to burn off, so if that's all you manage, and you add in a post-workout snack too, you could even find yourself gaining weight!

Q   What happens when you train while fasting?

A   Looking back to a study carried out by the US Army in 1988, there's no need to fear running out of glucose if you haven't eaten for a day. In fact, it seems to be possible to exercise for just as long after a three-and-a-half day- fast as it is after an overnight fast when working at a low intensity. Researchers in the same study found that blood glucose levels were maintained too.

In another small study published in the Journal of Physical Activity and Health, this time on healthy people who exercised at a relatively high intensity for an hour-and-a-half, fasting for 16–18 hours didn't impede their efforts. Interestingly, drinking a sports drink didn't make them feel or perform better either.

Meanwhile, researchers at Pennington Biomedical Research Center have discovered that consuming carbohydrates during exercise can actually decrease the expression of genes that are involved in fat metabolism. So, the more carbs you take in during exercise, the worse your body gets at tapping into its fat stores!

Sticking to plain water, or a calorie-free drink, increases the proportion of fat burned during exercise because less glucose is available. When you consume a sports drink, the glucose is rapidly delivered to your blood and provides an instant source of fuel. Without this, you need to tap into your body's fat stores.

Q   What's meant by "train low, race high"?

A   "Train low" means that some training is done without carbs to encourage the body to burn fat. As the bulk of modern sports nutrition research highlights the role of carbohydrates in enhancing performance under race conditions, the "race high" part involves taking on standard sports drinks or gels during events.

"Train low" training is different from simply training after an overnight fast, when muscle glycogen levels are still relatively high. Studies investigating the "train low" approach deplete participants' glycogen stores by putting them through an hour or more of aerobic training. After an hour's rest, participants then complete up to an hour of high-intensity exercise, all with only water to drink.

But be careful because training in a glycogen-depleted state has its risks.

These include increased levels of stress hormones, muscle breakdown, fatigue and lowered immune response. If, while fasting, you decide to add some endurance training to your schedule, especially at a high intensity, it's probably best, initially, to limit it to once a week. Allow plenty of time for recovery, and monitor your response, stopping if you feel unwell or fatigued.

FASTING FOR A STRONGER BODY

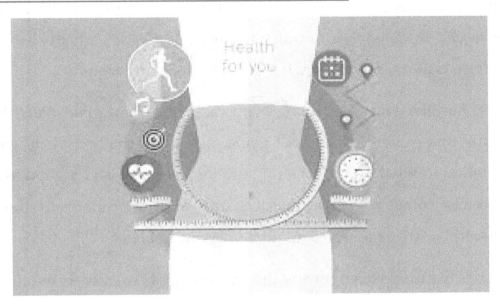

Weight-training enthusiasts use intermittent fasting as a technique to build lean mass and lose fat, with the goal of achieving a "shredded" or "ripped" physique. The explosion in popularity of intermittent fasting over the past few years is in part due to fitness experts such as Martin Berkhan, who designed the "Lean Gains" 16/8 hour fast. This method focuses the fast around the times you're scheduled to work out. The reason for this is that, in order to build muscle, you need to be in positive energy and protein balance after your workout, otherwise your muscles will be consumed for energy instead of getting bigger. Therefore, while the workout is done in the fasted state, the biggest meal of the day is right after the workout. Some people also take "branched-chain amino acid" supplements to maximize levels of growth hormone and to kick-start the muscle- building process.

FASTING AND MOTIVATION

The final motivator, when thinking about incorporating fasting with exercise, is that it could give you more energy to train. There are lots of arguments over whether diet or exercise is more important when it comes to losing weight.

You may be familiar with the saying "you can't out-train a bad diet". While it's probably true that exercise alone isn't going to get you the body you want if you pay no attention to what you eat, dieting without exercise isn't a good idea either. After all, exercise comes with an impressive array of health benefits itself from heart and lung health, to stress relief, to maintaining strong bones.

When it comes to muscle strength and the way you look, exercise is the clear winner over diet. Researchers at Ann Arbor University in Michigan looked at how women's bodies responded to diet alone versus exercise alone. They found that, as expected, diet was more effective at reducing body weight, but exercise was more effective when it came to losing fat and maintaining muscle.

The thing is, getting the motivation to exercise can be hard when you're "on a diet" because you're always eating less than you're burning off and you often feel like you just don't have the energy. The good thing about fasting is that the gaps between meals are longer so when you do eat, you get to eat more. This means that you can time your exercise around the times when you've eaten and are feeling energetic. You're more likely to work harder!

MEDITATION

For those with ambition above and beyond the physical benefits of fasting, getting into the fasting state of mind can be helped by meditation, and if you have the time and inclination at least once in your life, a week's retreat can take the fasting experience to another level.

Meditation can be viewed in scientific terms for its effects on the mind and the body. During meditation, a marked increase in blood flow slows heart rate, and high blood pressure drops to within normal ranges. Recent research indicates that meditation can also boost the immune system and reduce free radicals – in effect, a slowing down of the ageing process.

There's much talk about the power of meditation and how you can use your mind to manifest great piles of money. But, becoming more aware of your mind is not just about manipulating it or attempting only to have positive thoughts – rather, it's about the ability to direct your attention toward or away from the mind at will.

My most intensive fast was on a 10-day silent meditation retreat during my time in India. One evening, five days into the experience when I was seriously doubting my judgement about freezing my butt off in a cold cave in the Himalayas, I had what I've come to realize was a "breakthrough" moment. In spiritual terms I'd describe it as a moment of grace. With a raw, pure energy of infinite magnitude, my mind flashed through formative experiences – good and bad – that had shaped my life. As my mind was swept along on this emotional rollercoaster, my body conveniently left the room, leaving me nowhere to run or hide… or at least that was how it felt!

When I first started to meditate, I tried too hard. Furiously studying the science of the mind or contorting your face into Zen-like expressions won't work. The only way to experience meditation is actually to experience it. It can be maddening. You'll be trying to meditate for hours and then, just when you're ready to give up, you might get a flash of something akin to what you were aiming for. Yet, in that momentary shift you might see how you could choose to do a few things differently, or how some really small things have a huge impact on you, and how easy it would be to make a few minor changes. Many great thinkers have talked about breakthroughs and inspiration. The most famous of all was probably Albert Einstein, who said that no problem can be solved from the same level of consciousness that created it.

So, if you do manage to get your mind to stop its usual chatter through meditation, try asking yourself a question when all is calm. For example, if you always react to something uncomfortable by quashing the emotion with food, then meditation can create a gap to ask why. Sometimes there's a clear answer to that question, and sometimes there isn't. Usually, it takes a bit of time.

YOGA

Yoga is often lumped together with meditation since the kind of person who likes yoga is often into meditation, and vice versa. For people with a poor attention span, yoga can be a good way of getting into a calm state without the need ever to sit cross-legged.

There are many forms of yoga and it's a case of having a go and seeing which suits you best. Regardless of which tradition you choose, good yoga teachers can make you walk out of the class feeling a foot taller and ready to take on the world. My advice would be:

• If you're gentle by nature, try Hatha.

• If you're into precision and detail, go for Iyengar.

• If you like the spiritual side of yoga, opt for Sivananda.

• If you want yoga to help you sleep, try Yin.

• If you're fit and physical, Ashtanga or Vinyasa "flow" yoga will be more your bag.

• If you really want to sweat, try Bikram, or "hot yoga". It's not for the faint hearted and has some medical contra-indications, but it's considered seriously addictive by devotees.

ANTI-AGING TIPS FOR FASTING

There are far too many tips which would enable you achieve that anti-aging look and feel. However, we are going to be grouping them for you to easily process and remember.

EAT WELL

The problem with most fasting information is that it only focuses on the fasting bit, not on what you need to eat. If you're eating fewer calories, what you do eat becomes even more important. Why? We need nutrients for the glands and organs of the body to thrive and burn fat. Restricting nutrients by living on processed foods can deprive the body of the essential vitamins, minerals, fats and proteins it needs to maintain a healthy immune system, recover from injury or illness, keep muscles strong and maintain the metabolism. That's why this book includes these nutrition rules and practical fasting plans and recipes to help guide you.

RULE 1: ONLY EAT "REAL" FOOD

This means no fake food and no diet-drinks. If you grew up in the UK, chances are you'll have fond memories of bright orange corn snacks and fizzy drinks that turned your tongue red or blue. It's to be hoped that now you're "all grown up 'n' stuff", you eat lots of rocket and Parmesan salads, roasted artichoke and monkfish. If only that was the case for all of us. Celebrity chefs may make out that this is the norm but it just isn't. Most people still eat a diet full of processed, refined, low-fiber, nutrient-deficient foods.

Not all processed food is bad, though. In fact, some of it's great. Canned food without added sugar or salt and freshly-frozen fruit and veg are just a couple of examples of stellar staples for your larder. It's the low-calorie, low-fat, oh-so-easy snacks and meals that you need to watch out for since they're often loaded with chemicals and hidden sugars.

Heavily processed foods can also be high in chemicals. There's a real and present danger that chemicals in the environment may have a blocking effect on hormones that control weight loss. When the brain is affected by toxins, it's possible that hormone signaling is impaired. The reason why we're unsure as to the extent of the problem is that it's impossible to test for the thousands of chemicals that are contributing to the "cocktail" effect on the body. Err on the side of caution and control what you can. Keep foods "real"!

But what makes up a real-food diet?

PROTEIN

Protein is made up of amino acids, often called the "building blocks of life", and we need all of them to stay alive and thrive. Proteins from animal sources – meat, dairy, fish and eggs – contain all the amino acids and are therefore classed as "complete" proteins. Soya beans also fall into this category. Once and for all, eggs are healthy. Eggs have had a tough time of it over the years. First the salmonella scare, then the unfair link to cholesterol. Eggs are low in saturated fat and if you eat eggs in the morning, you're less likely to feel hungry later in the day.

Vegetable sources provide incomplete proteins. If you're vegetarian or vegan, you'll get your protein from nuts, seeds, legumes and grains but you need a good variety of these to ensure that you get the full range of essential amino acids.

TOP TIP:

• Include more beans and lentils in your meals. Examples include kidney beans, butter beans, chickpeas or red and green lentils. They're rich in protein and contain complex carbohydrates, which provide slow and sustained energy release. They also contain fiber, which may help to control your blood fats. Try adding them to stews, casseroles, soups and salads.

CARBOHYDRATES

Carbs are one of the most controversial topics in nutrition and weight loss. For years we've been told that we eat too much fat, and that saturated fat is the main cause of heart disease. But recently, some experts have challenged this view, suggesting that carbohydrate is responsible for the obesity epidemic and a whole host of diseases. Should we cut carbs, avoid fat or simply reduce our food intake and exercise more?

When the body is starved of carbohydrates it looks for energy in its glycogen stores. Water binds to every gram of glycogen so it's easy to get dramatic weight loss – the only problem is that it's mostly water weight! Along with those glycogen stores you'll begin to lose fat but not at a rate higher than a healthier (and easier) weight-loss method.

The truth is there are healthy fats and healthy carbohydrates. Avoiding carbs altogether is unnecessary and potentially dangerous. The key is in recognizing that not all carbs are created equal. Low glycemic index (GI) carbohydrates, found in fiber-rich fruits, beans, unrefined grains and vegetables, are important for good health and can actively support weight loss – for example, through reducing appetite and energy intake.

However, high-GI refined carbohydrates, such as those found in soft drinks, white bread, pastries, certain breakfast cereals and sweeteners, not only make it harder to lose weight but could damage long-term health. Studies show that eating a lot of high-GI carbohydrates can increase the risk of heart disease and Type-2 diabetes.

There's been a lot of research on low-carbohydrate diets in recent years. It was initially thought that they may damage bone and kidney health, but this doesn't seem to be the case unless you have a pre-existing kidney problem. Lowcarb diets can be effective for weight loss and also improve risk factors for heart disease and diabetes. However, they do carry risks.

First, the low intake of fruit, vegetables and whole grains on a lowcarb diet reduces the intake of certain vitamins and minerals, notably folate, which is vital for women who may become pregnant. Second, cutting out unrefined carbohydrates dramatically reduces the amount of fiber in the diet, which leads to constipation and changes the balance of gut bacteria. In the long term, this may increase the risk of colorectal cancer. Finally, eating a lowcarb diet based on animal protein has been associated with a significantly higher risk of mortality. High levels of meat and dairy create substances called prostaglandins, which are inflammatory. Inflammation is bad news for the body. Side-effects of a very lowcarb diet can include bad breath, hair loss, mood swings, constipation and fatigue. In my opinion, this is too high a price to pay when weight loss can be achieved just as quickly without the side-effects.

For this reason, while I'd never recommend cutting out carbohydrates as a food group, my recipes focus on unrefined, low-GI carbs from whole foods rather than refined, high-GI carbs. As well as improving health, low-GI carbs release glucose into the bloodstream more slowly, which leads to a more sustained energy release, rather than the peaks and crashes you tend to experience if you eat a lot of high-GI carbs.

TOP TIP:

•   Eat bulky carbs to become slim. When you choose "big" foods like fruits, vegetables, salads and soups, which are bulked up by fiber and water, you're eating a lot of food that fills you up, but not a lot of calories.

FAT

Since fat is the greatest source of calories, eating less of it can help you to lose weight. However, fat is actually a vital nutrient and is an important part of your diet because it supplies the essential fatty acids needed for vitamin absorption, healthy skin, growth and the regulation of bodily functions. In fact, eating too little fat can actually cause a number of health problems.

The right kinds of fat, in the right amounts, can also help you to feel fuller for longer, so try not to think of fat as your mortal diet enemy, but rather a useful ally in the pursuit of your healthier lifestyle! Adding a little fat to your meals helps your body absorb nutrients and enhances the flavor of your food, so recipes have been created with this in mind. Choose monounsaturated fats or oils (e.g., olive oil and rapeseed oil) as these types of fats are better for your heart. Coconut oil can be a good choice for cooking as it's heat-stable.

TOP TIPS:

• Increase essential fats – aim for at least two portions of oily fish a week. Examples include mackerel, sardines, salmon and pilchards. Oily fish contains a type of polyunsaturated fat called omega 3, which helps protect against heart disease. If you don't eat fish, use flaxseed oil in salad dressing and snack on walnuts.

• If you use butter, stick to a thin scraping on bread and just a smidgen for flavor in cooking.

• Choose lean meat and fish as low-fat alternatives to fatty meats.

• Choose lower-fat dairy foods such as skimmed or semi-skimmed milk and reduced-fat natural yogurt.

• Grill, poach, steam or oven bake instead of frying or cooking with oil or other fats.

• Watch out for creamy sauces and dressings – swap them for tomato-based sauces. Add herbs, lemon, spices and garlic to reduced-fat meals to boost flavor.

• Use cheese as a topping, not a meal – in other words, no macaroni cheese! Choose cheese with a strong flavor, such as Parmesan or goat's cheese so that you only need to use a small amount.

RULE 2: CUT OUT SUGAR

Too much sugar makes you fat and has an ageing effect on the skin. Sugar links with collagen and elastin and reduces the elasticity of the skin, making you look older than your years. The recipes I provide use low-sugar fruits to add a little sweetness – and the occasional drizzle of a natural sweetener such as honey is fine – but, in general, sugar is bad news and best avoided.

TOP TIP:

• Stick to dark chocolate if you need a chocolate "fix" (which simply is the case sometimes!), as most people need less of it to feel satisfied.

RULE 3: WATCH THE ALCOHOL

Over the years the alcohol content of most drinks has gone up. A drink can now have more units than you think. A small glass of wine (175ml/5½fl cup) could be as much as two units. Remember, alcohol contains empty calories so think about cutting back further if you're trying to lose weight. That's a maximum of two units of alcohol per day for a woman and three units per day for a man. For example, a single pub measure (25ml/¾fl oz) of spirit is about one unit, and a half pint of lager, ale, bitter or cider is one to one-and-a-half units.

TOP TIP:

• If you're out for the evening, try out some healthy soft drinks such as tonic with cordial, or an alcohol-free grape juice as a tasty substitute to wine. Alcohol-free beers are also becoming increasingly popular and are available in most pubs and bars.

RULE 4: EAT FRUIT, DON'T DRINK IT

If you consume around 1 liter (35fl oz/4 cups) fruit juice, remember you'll be imbibing 500 calories. That's fine if you're juice fasting, but too much if it's simply a snack. You could tuck into a baked potato with tuna and two pieces of fruit for the same number of calories.

TOP TIPS:

- Choose herbal teas (especially green tea, which may aid fat loss).

- Feel free to have a cup or two of tea or coffee. A small amount of milk is allowed but keep it to a splash when you're fasting.

- Sip water throughout the fast, aiming for a fluid intake of around 1.2–2 liters (40–70fl oz/4¾–8 cups) a day. This will not only help to keep hunger pangs at bay, it will also keep you hydrated.

RULE 5: AVOID THE PITFALLS

TOP TIPS:

• Top up before you fast. When you first start fasting, you may feel hungry during the times when you'd normally have a meal and you may also feel slightly light-headed if you have sugary foods as your last meal. This isn't a sign that you're wasting away or entering starvation mode, and these feelings of hunger will usually subside once that usual meal time has passed. Try to get your carbohydrate intake from fruit, vegetables and whole grains and eat a good amount of protein, which will fill you up for longer. Following the fasting plans will make this as straightforward as possible.

• Stock up for quick meals. Make sure you always have ingredients in your fridge and cupboards for meals that can be put together quickly, such as stir- fries, soups and salads.

• Don't polish off the kids' plates. Eating the children's leftovers is a fast track to weight gain for parents. Put the plates straight into the sink or dishwasher when the children have finished their meal, so you won't be tempted!

• Downsize your dinner plate. Much of our hunger and satiation is psychological. If we see a huge plate only half full, we'll feel like we haven't eaten enough. But if the plate is small but completely filled, we'll subconsciously feel that we have eaten enough.

• Beware of the Frappuccino effect. Black coffee only contains about 10 calories but a milky coffee can contain anything from 100 calories for a standard small cappuccino to a whopping 350+ calories for a Grande with all the trimmings. Much like the plate size, shrink your cup size and shrink your waist line. Don't be afraid to ask for half the milk – spell it out: "Don't fill up the cup." I do it all the time and the best baristas get it right first time!

•　　The sandwich has become the ubiquitous carb-laden "lunch on the go". Lose the top piece of bread to cut your refined carbohydrates and instead fill up with a small bag of green salad leaves and healthy dressing.

•　　Don't try to change everything at once. Bad habits are hard enough to break as it is. Focus on breaking one at a time.

•　　If you're a parent, choose your meal skipping wisely. I've tried fasting with a toddler who doesn't understand why Mummy isn't eating and will, quite literally, shove a fistful of tuna pasta into my mouth.

•　　Get the portions right. If you're restricting the number of meals you're having, it makes sense that the portion sizes need to be bigger than they would be if you were eating five mini-meals a day. Use the recipe section as a guide to how big your portions should be.

FASTING SAFELY

By now I hope that you have an open mind to the many benefits of fasting and that you're excited about giving it a go. If you've read this book and are still trying to decide if, when, or how to give fasting a try, remember that you'll only ever truly "get it" by trying it for yourself.

Before you launch headlong into your new fasting lifestyle, here are a few words of caution. Although fasting has been around for millennia, the science on how and when to fast is in its early stages. For example, there's very little research on how fasting affects fertility.

There are some people who should avoid fasting completely, some who should seek medical advice first, and some situations where it might not be right for you. Fasting isn't something that you should just jump into, and it doesn't suit everyone.

WHEN NOT TO FAST

You should avoid fasting if any of the following apply:

• You are pregnant, breastfeeding, or actively trying for a baby (it's okay to fast if you're getting your body ready to conceive, but please don't consider fasting if there's any chance you could already be pregnant).

• You have ever experienced an eating disorder.

• You are underweight

You should seek medical advice first if any of the following apply:

• You have a long-term medical condition such as cancer, diabetes, ulcerative colitis, epilepsy, anemia, liver, kidney or lung disease.

• You have a condition that affects your immune system.

• You are on medication, particularly medicines that control your blood sugar, blood pressure or blood lipids (cholesterol).

POSSIBLE SIDE-EFFECTS AND HOW TO MANAGE THEM

As we learnt earlier in the book, fasting may make you feel a bit "yucky" at first. Many juice fasters experience headaches through caffeine withdrawal, and feeling hungry is natural when you first try a fast. These effects don't usually last long, and most people find that they're outweighed by the positive effects of fasting.

More serious side-effects may include:

- Dehydration or over-hydration.

- Feeling dizzy or light-headed.

- Extreme fatigue.

- Constipation.

- Nausea or vomiting.

- Insomnia.

- Irregular periods.

Always err on the side of caution and stop the fast if you don't feel well. You can minimize the risk of some side-effects by approaching the fast safely.

Keto Electrolytes - Do You Need Electrolytes On Keto Diet?

What is keto diet or ketogenic diet?

Keto diet is one of the best and most useful methods to shed weight and have relief of over weightiness. The keto diet has many benefits for people with lots of fats and helps them improve health and spirit. It is also referred to as ketogenic diet.

The ketogenic diet is a very low carb, high fat diet that shares many similarities with the Atkins and low carb diets. It involves drastically reducing carbohydrate intake and replacing it with fat. This reduction in carbs puts your body into a metabolic state called ketosis. When this happens, your body becomes incredibly efficient at burning fat for energy. It also turns fat into ketones in the liver, which can supply energy for the brain.

Ketogenic diets can cause significant reductions in blood sugar and insulin levels. This, along with the increased ketones, has some health benefits.

How it can shed weight and also cause dehydration?

Keto diet can reduce weight by removing fats as it is a high fat diet where it is also a low carb diet. Basically the keto diet utilizes most of the fats as an energy and power source where it causes reduction in fats and thus there is loss in weight as well.

There's evidence that ketogenic diets can help with weight loss.

They may help you lose fat, preserve muscle mass, and improve many markers of disease. Some studies have suggested that a ketogenic diet may be more effective than a low fat diet for weight loss, even after matching the total calorie intake.

In one older study, people on a ketogenic diet lost 2.2 times more weight than those on a low calorie, low fat diet. Triglyceride and HDL (good) cholesterol levels also improved .However, both groups reduced calorie consumption by a comparable amount, and this may have increased weight loss.

Another 2007 study compared a low carb diet to the Diabetes UK's dietary guidelines. It found the low-carb group lost 15.2 pounds (6.9 kg), while the low fat group lost only 4.6 pounds (2.1 kg). Over 3 months, the low-carb diet caused 3 times more weight loss .

However, there was no difference in HbA1c, ketone, or lipid levels between the groups. Also, those on the low-carb diet also decreased their calorie intake. Finally, there was no difference in fat or protein intake between the two groups. This is important to note if people are increasing their fat intake because they are following a keto diet.

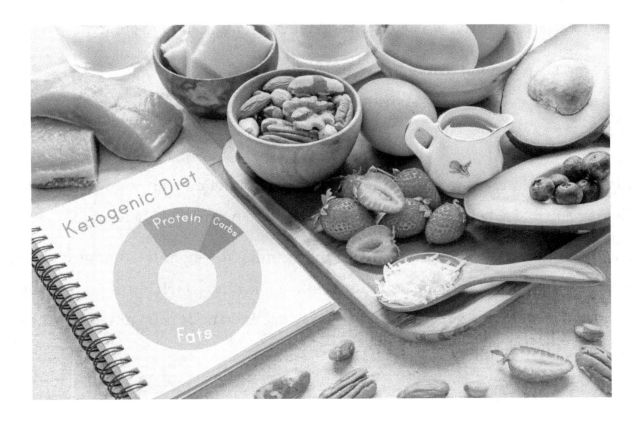

However, there are contrasting theories for these findings. Some researchers argue the results are simply due to a higher protein intake, and others think there's a distinct "metabolic advantage" to ketogenic diets.

Other ketogenic diet studies have found that the ketogenic diet may lead to reductions in appetite and food intake. This is extremely important when applying the research to a real-life setting.If you dislike counting calories, the data suggests a ketogenic diet may be a good option for you. You can eliminate certain foods and don't have to track calories.

If you follow the keto diet, you still have to check labels and keep track of your total grams of carbs each day, which requires paying attention to food choices.

However, keep in mind that many of the studies mentioned above had small sample sizes and only evaluated the short-term effects of the diet.

Additional research is needed to determine how the diet may impact weight loss in the long run and whether weight is regained once a normal diet is resumed.

Scientifically the keto diet has shown better results in weight loss but also during the process when on keto, the body turns into a machine which burns fats so that is why it causes dehydration as well. as the body needs water to calm down but during the process it is dehydrated.

How it promotes weight loss:

Here's how ketogenic diets promote weight loss:

Higher protein intake. Some ketogenic diets lead to an increase in protein intake, which has many weight loss benefits.

Gluconeogenesis. Your body converts fat and protein into carbs for fuel. This process may burn many additional calories each day.

Appetite suppressant. Ketogenic diets help you feel full. This is supported by positive changes in hunger hormones, including leptin and ghrelin.

Improved insulin sensitivity. Ketogenic diets can drastically improve insulin sensitivity, which can help improve fuel utilization and metabolism.

Decreased fat storage. Some research suggests ketogenic diets may reduce lip genesis, the process of converting sugar into fat. This is because excess carbs are stored as fat. When there's a minimal intake of carbs, fat is used for energy.

Increased fat burning. Several studies have found that ketogenic diets may slightly increase the amount of fat you burn during rest, daily activity, and exercise, although more research is needed.

In these ways, a ketogenic diet can be effective at helping you lose weight.

However, note that it's important to ensure that you're meeting your calorie needs when following the ketogenic diet. Cutting calories too much can slow your metabolism, making it harder to lose weight in the long run.

Some experts also note that, while the keto diet may lead to weight loss in the short term, the loss is unlikely to continue. It can also be hard to follow the diet for a long time.

What electrolytes do you need on a ketogenic diet?

Electrolytes are our body where they are needed for our daily life functions like heart functioning ability, brain activity and many others.

In the context of nutrition, electrolytes are essential minerals that carry an electrical charge. The most popular examples include sodium, magnesium and potassium. Chemically, electrolytes are substances that produce an electrically conducting solution when dissolved in water.

In the body, electrolytes play a vital role in supporting cell function, producing energy and stimulating muscle contractions.

They literally keep the human heart beating.

Maintaining sufficient levels of electrolytes through nutrition is vital, regardless of whether or not you're on keto. But many people fail to consume sufficient amounts of micronutrients.

There are many reasons for this, such as food choices (including what they don't eat), soil nutrient depletion (many modern crops have fewer nutrients than in the past), and lifestyle factors like smoking or eating disorders.

When you start on a ketogenic diet, some of those nutritional gaps get amplified and exposed — particularly if your body is used to burning glucose (from the carbs you've been eating) as its primary fuel source.

Keto electrolytes are the most important in the diet, as electrolytes in the keto diet have many important functions.

Main electrolytes in keto diet are;

1. Sodium

2. Potassium

3. Calcium

4. Magnesium

These are the main keto electrolytes and they are needed for a Ketogenic diet.

Keto flu

Keto electrolytes as explained are the main major things if there are no sufficient amounts of electrolytes in the body and the diet is not proper then it may cause the Keto flu. And due to this keto flue many problems begin to exist and may cause so severe health condition problems like;

- Sleeping difficulty
- Headache
- Brain fog
- Irritability

- Fatigue
- Laziness

How to know if the keto electrolytes level is dropping in the keto diet?

Main four electrolytes has its own effects on deficiency Sodium, Magnesium, Potassium and calcium cause different problems like;

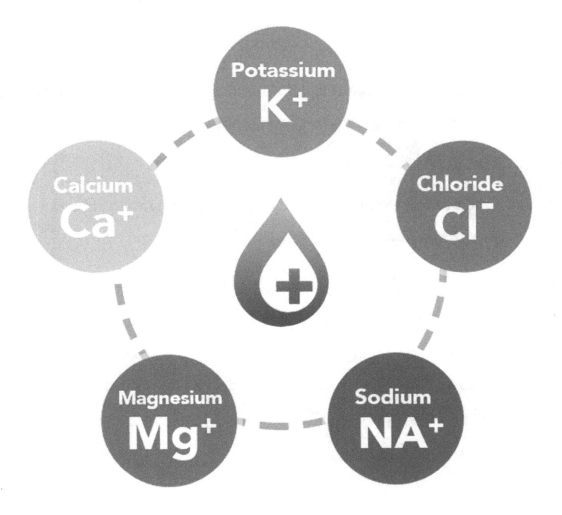

Deficiency in electrolytes may cause the following problems;

1. Sodium

Deficiency of sodium in keto electrolyte diet may cause fatigue, weakness, headache and difficulty concentrating.

2. Magnesium

Deficiency of Magnesium in keto electrolyte diet may cause muscle cramping or twitching of body parts either at night or day time. Also after exercise the body parts may twitch.

3. Potassium

Deficiency of Potassium in keto electrolyte diet may cause Muscle cramps, Muscle twitching, Heart palpitations / increased awareness of heartbeat.

4. Calcium

Deficiency of Calcium in keto electrolyte diet may cause dental problems, muscles contractions, osteoporosis and cataracts.

Replenish With Keto Electrolyte Drinks

Keto electrolyte drink has so much energy and can decrease the deficiency of the electrolytes in the ketogenic diet. These drinks are made from natural herbs and vegetables. Most of the daily life fluid contains electrolytes and they can replenish the electrolytes in keto diet plan.

Such drinks may include the following;

1.   <u>Electrolyte-infused waters</u>

Electrolyte infused water is one of the best electrolytes replenishing water as it is full of electrolytes and also keeps the body hydrated all the time.

These electrolytes may consist of sugar which is the main source of energy and gives more power to the body and keeps it hydrated as well.

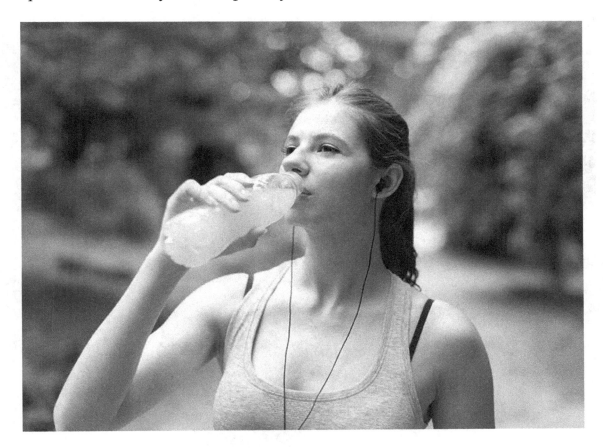

2.   Watermelon water

Juice from watermelon is simple water from watermelon but it is not just water it fills the necessary electrolytes which are needed for the human body and also in the keto electrolyte diet plan.

Such water drinks fill all the needs and also the main elements in the body for keto diet.

As most of it contains potassium and magnesium as well.

3.   Black or green tea

Tea is a natural option that contains a negligible number of carbs — typically less than 1 gram per cup (240 mL). You can enjoy it iced or hot. Black tea is made from aged tea leaves, giving it a more robust flavor, darker color, and higher caffeine content. Meanwhile, green tea is made from fresh tea leaves, lending it a more floral flavor, lighter color, and less caffeine.

You can also choose white tea, which is made from young tea leaves. It has a very mild, delicate flavor compared with both black and green tea. Furthermore, tea is essentially calorie-free and full of polyphenol antioxidants. For example, green tea is rich in epigallocatechin gallate (EGCG), a powerful antioxidant that may provide anticancer benefits.

4.   KETO LEMON GINGER ELECTROLYTE DRINK

Lemons are not only high in Vitamin C but also antioxidants which can help boost the immune system to fight against germs that cause colds and flu. Ginger is also an antioxidant, anti inflammatory, antibacterial and antiviral.

Replenish With Keto Electrolyte Foods

In keto electrolyte diet make sure the daily intake of the foods contains those which may help you replenish the electrolytes and help you gain more energy. While these foods are listed below and they can help you have the restored energy back.

While some of the electrolyte replenishing foods may include:

1. Fatty fish

In keto electrolyte, when there is a need to replenish it fatty fish is the great source of getting a great amount of electrolytes as it is a great source of protein and It also has omega 3's, thus it helps a lot as it has a great amount of electrolytes.

2. Dark Green Leafy Veg and Other Non-Starchy Vegetables

Keto diet needs electrolytes daily, well foods like vegetables have great potential in it. All the vegetables are a great source of proteins, calcium, and magnesium as well. Daily intake of it helps to increase the electrolytes level in the body.

3. Bone Broth

Bone broth is made by simmering the bones and connective tissue of animals. The mineral content is extremely high and having one cup a day can significantly help with the symptoms of the keto flu. It is an especially good source of naturally occurring sodium making it even better for the body.

Bone broth – on average 1 cup contains 120 mg of magnesium, 528 mg of potassium and 1,104 mg of sodium (values vary per each batch and depend on the bones and the amount of salt used).

How to include bone broth in your diet:

- Easy Low-Carb Vietnamese Pho

- Low-Carb Duck Ramen

- The Best Instant Pot Chicken Noodle Soup

4.   Cacao Powder and Dark Chocolate

Dark chocolate (above 70% cocoa content) has been shown to contain compounds that have many health benefits to the body. Surprisingly to some, it is also packed with some key minerals and electrolytes.

Whilst a whole bar could significantly contribute to you RDA of magnesium and potassium, it can also add considerably to your total carbohydrate content. Sticking to 1-2 squares of good quality chocolate will be enough to reap the benefits.

A 1-oz/ 28 gram serving contains:

- dark chocolate - 40-70 mg of magnesium and 200-540 mg of potassium (values vary in 70%-100% chocolate, the more cacao solids the better)
- 1 tbsp cacao powder - 24 mg of magnesium and 69 mg of potassium

How to include dark chocolate in your diet:

- Keto Chocolate Pots with Chocolate Curls
- Healthy Low-Carb Double Chocolate Brownies
- Super Creamy Keto Chocolate Ice-Cream

How to Select an Electrolyte Supplement

As is the case with most supplements, the market is flooded with electrolyte products. That makes it challenging to pick one that's effective and that properly supports your lifestyle.

I've tried dozens of different products and wanted to share my advice on how to pick a good supplement.

Generally speaking, I look at the following attributes when shopping for electrolytes:

Primary ingredients and their dosage

Type of minerals (chemical structure)

Bioavailability (how much of the supplement can be used for normal body function)

Other ingredients (such as artificial sweeteners or fillers)

Price

Delivery form (powder or liquid)

The first thing I look for is what minerals the product has and what the dosage and chemical structure is.

Many products on the market have such low doses of sodium, magnesium and potassium that they're practically ineffective.

It's also important to understand that there are often different versions (molecular structures) of certain minerals, such as magnesium and potassium. Both the bioavailability and absorbability can vary greatly between those different types.

When selecting a powdered product, I try to stick with electrolytes that are easily absorbed and don't have a laxative effect, including:

- Sodium chloride (salt)
- Magnesium citrate
- Potassium chloride

It's also worth noting that there's a difference between obtaining certain electrolytes from real food compared to from a supplement. The magnesium found in certain foods (like spinach) is much better absorbed (and has a higher bioavailability) than any powdered magnesium you'll find.

The good news is that there are certain liquid supplements on the market that provide nature-identical electrolytes from plant-based sources (see below).

It's also important to carefully look at the list of "other ingredients" when shopping for a supplement.

That list often contains a bunch of crap ingredients you don't want to put into your body, including:

Added sugars

Artificial colors or sweeteners (i.e., sucralose)

Unnecessary fillers and flow agents

Ineffective proprietary blends

Last but not least, I look at the price. The problem is that you have to take potency and serving sizes into account to find out whether a product is reasonably priced or not.

CONCLUSION

If you've read this book and are still trying to decide if, when or how to give fasting a try, stop! Don't intellectualize or rationalize it. You'll only ever truly "get it" by trying for yourself.

It is a leap of faith to believe that something as simple as drinking juice can do what pills and potions cannot. So, you just need to make the leap and see what happens.

You need to remember that healing from the inside is something your body is designed to do. If you create the right conditions, the body will respond. Fasting can create the right internal environment for healing and positive change to occur.

The same process happens emotionally, too. There is nothing quite like the perspective or creative leap that occurs in the mind when you take time out from your norm. Just imagine what life could be like if you followed your dreams.

I know because that is exactly what happened to me. Before I end this book, I want to tell you the story of the TV series that first spread the word of the power of fasting. It's something I am asked about all the time, all over the world, and it's a story I've never told fully before now.

I admitted at the beginning of the book that I kind of stumbled upon fasting. I had already studied Nutritional Medicine so I had a good grounding in the science of sound eating. However, when I started using juice fasting, first on my own and then with clients, the results were so astonishing that it was the push I needed to give up a six-figure salary, sell a house and drive to Spain with nothing more than the notion of following my dream to set up my first juice- fasting retreat.

One year later I had learned the local lingo, made lifelong friends and was enjoying a wonderful lifestyle of yoga on the beach, tapas and siestas. Alas, my dwindling bank balance told a different story. I had hired a rustic villa in the mountains to run juice retreats for a few people at a time, working from dawn till dusk and doing everything myself – not exactly a sustainable business model.

A random email from an old TV contact was the reality check I needed to put the retreats – and fasting – on the map. I worked up a pitch document and decided to knock on the doors of any media person I knew to get the format made into a TV series. Thirteen knock-backs later and I finally got a "yes".

My retreats ended up becoming the subject of more than seven TV series, shown in over 22 countries around the world, which continue to be shown today.

I believe that the reason the series became such a phenomenon is that it showed, beyond a shadow of a doubt, that even dramatic health conditions are curable.

Almost a decade on, I still have people from all over the world getting in touch or attending my retreats who say that watching the series gave them hope and a new direction. Many times, over I've been told that seeing health transformed using something as simple as a fast was the nudge they needed to take action in their own lives.

CPSIA information can be obtained
at www.ICGtesting.com
Printed in the USA
BVHW050309090721
611459BV00011B/467